D0070189

PERSPECTIVE

RELATED BOOKS BY THE AUTHOR. . .

Bounce: Living the Resilient Life (OUP)
Streams of Contentment (Sorin Books)
Riding the Dragon (Sorin Books)
The Inner Life of the Counselor (Wiley)
Primer on Posttraumatic Growth—Written with Mary Beth Werdel (Wiley)

ADVANCE PRAISE FOR *PERSPECTIVE: THE CALM WITHIN THE STORM*

This is the kind of book you can't put down because it is so necessary: gentle, wise, erudite advice on how to slow down and notice the uncertainty and beauty of life. I read it in one hungry helping, underlining frantically, phoning up friends to read them quotes. I know that I will return to it often.

ALEXANDRA FULLER
AUTHOR, *Cocktail Hour under the Tree of Forgetfulness*

Dr. Wicks unlocks the secret to achieving the fullest potential in each of us. I wish I had read this book 30 years ago and had assigned it to everyone under my command. Perspective: The Calm within the Storm *guides us to be more positive, focused, and open-minded—shaping a state of mind where each of us will succeed!*

MIKE GOULD, LIEUTENANT GENERAL (RETIRED), USAF
SUPERINTENDENT, UNITED STATES AIR FORCE ACADEMY,
JUNE 2009-AUGUST 2013

Robert Wicks leads us on an inward exploration designed to foster our own personal journey toward enlightenment by opening the door to pathways for living and being that have always been there right before our eyes, but perhaps previously not readily accessible to us. Wicks opens these doors for the willing participant, offering us the possibility of achieving our full potential and living life more richly, in a more rewarding, fulfilling, and meaningful manner. The key is to join him on this journey of perspective that he masterfully leads within the pages of this book.

JEFFREY E. BARNETT, PSY.D., ABPP
PAST PRESIDENT, DIVISION OF PSYCHOTHERAPY,
AMERICAN PSYCHOLOGICAL ASSOCIATION

Robert Wicks has written a truly remarkable book for leading a more meaningful, balanced, resilient life. His ability to tie together and apply different theories, including those related to mindfulness, positive psychology, cognitive behavioral therapy, happiness, and posttraumatic growth is very impressive. Dr. Wicks skillfully draws from these perspectives to provide realistic, practical strategies that we all can use to adopt a more positive, healthy outlook and lifestyle. He does so in a reader-friendly, nonjudgmental, empathic manner, which makes it easier to understand, appreciate, and apply his ideas. This book will be read and re-read by those seeking to experience a life that is more enriching and purposeful. It will also serve as a valuable resource by therapists/counselors both in their professional and personal lives.

ROBERT BROOKS, PH.D., FACULTY, HARVARD MEDICAL SCHOOL; CO-AUTHOR, *The Power of Resilience*

This book is a lovely, clear, and inspiring read. Using personal examples combined with the insights of Eastern spiritual traditions and clinical psychology, the author guides the reader through easy-to-follow steps to develop a healthier perspective on life.

KRISTIN NEFF, PH.D.
AUTHOR, *Self-Compassion*; ASSOCIATE PROFESSOR, UNIVERSITY OF TEXAS

Perspective: The Calm within the Storm *is the type of gift that keeps giving. Wherever you are on your journey, this book is your perfect companion. I feel wiser and richer because of it. My wish for you is a willingness to receive and start reading in order to discover the tools you need to create your own umbrella to weather the storms that come with life.*

FRANCOISE ADAN, M.D.
MEDICAL DIRECTOR, CONNOR INTEGRATIVE MEDICINE NETWORK, UNIVERSITY HOSPITALS

Perspective

The Calm within the Storm

ROBERT J. WICKS

Author of *Bounce: Living the Resilient Life*

OXFORD
UNIVERSITY PRESS

Oxford University Press is a department of the University of Oxford.
It furthers the University's objective of excellence in research, scholarship,
and education by publishing worldwide.

Oxford New York
Auckland Cape Town Dar es Salaam Hong Kong Karachi
Kuala Lumpur Madrid Melbourne Mexico City Nairobi
New Delhi Shanghai Taipei Toronto

With offices in
Argentina Austria Brazil Chile Czech Republic France Greece
Guatemala Hungary Italy Japan Poland Portugal Singapore
South Korea Switzerland Thailand Turkey Ukraine Vietnam

Published in the United States of America by
Oxford University Press
198 Madison Avenue, New York, NY 10016

Library of Congress Cataloging-in-Publication Data
Wicks, Robert J.
Perspective : the calm within the storm / by Robert J. Wicks.
pages cm
Includes bibliographical references and index.
ISBN 978–0–19–994455–2
1. Attitude (Psychology) 2. Perspective (Philosophy) 3. Meditation. I. Title.
BF327.W53 2014
158.1—dc23
2013028104

3 5 7 9 8 6 4 2
Printed in the United States of America
on acid-free paper

For Sue and Doug Ferraro, whose faithful friendship, compassionate presence, natural wisdom, and great sense of humor continue to inspire and help me gain a healthier sense of perspective

CONTENTS

THE PSYCHOLOGICAL PEARL OF GREAT PRICE: A PROLOGUE

Wish not for wealth or power
but for the passion of possibility,
for the eye, eternally young,
eternally ardent, that sees
possibility everywhere.
Søren Kierkegaard, *Either/Or*

When someone gains or regains a healthy sense of perspective, it feels like pure magic. The person sees more clearly and experiences greater freedom. Unforeseen possibility surfaces. New peace and joy are seeded.

The situation hasn't changed. Unwanted occurrences aren't denied or minimized: Instead, they are faced and explored differently—not with unrealistic expectations or the projection of blame, harshness, or self-recrimination, but with a sense of *intrigue.* There is a realization that whatever "darkness," suffering, confusion, or potentially addictive attraction may be present in the moment, it is not the end of the story. It is not the last word.

And so, having the passion and tools to continually seek out a healthier perspective is not simply a good idea. No, it is much more than that. It is actually a determining factor as to how life can be enjoyed more completely and shared more fully every minute of one's day. Having a healthy perspective is tantamount to possessing the psychological pearl of great price. Yet, as we shall see, this "pearl" may not be what we think it is.

THE CLASSIC AND CONTEMPORARY CALL TO HONOR PERSPECTIVE

Knowing the importance of perspective, recognizing more quickly when its guiding sense has temporarily slipped from our hands, and having the energy to seek it anew represents the key to a happy, meaningful, and naturally compassionate life. Classic and contemporary psychology have long known this and sought to provide potent portals to perspective. Psychology also now points to the findings of both quantitative and qualitative studies to assist in appreciating what really works in the search for a healthy perspective. Intense interest in the search for a way to open ourselves to life—which is enhancing yet often elusive—didn't begin with the behavioral sciences.

Encouragement to live life as a continual pilgrimage in search of a perspective that opens us up to life in new and renewing ways (so we don't get trapped in trivial or unhelpful cultural norms) begins with the early wisdom literature. For instance, in the *Talmud* we are cautioned, "You do not see things as they are. You see things as *you* are." In the Christian *New Testament* we read, "If your eye is good, your whole body will be good" (Matt. 6:22). The Buddhists speak about a true perspective as the unobstructed vision, and the Hindus refer to it in the *Upanishads* as a turning around in one's seat of consciousness.

Even in the brief maxims or sayings of ancient religious leaders, we see this call to let go, see differently, and live with greater dignity—even in the smallest actions of our life. For example, we can feel the theme of perspective breathing behind the urging of the Prophet Muhammad when he once reportedly quipped, "If you have enough money to buy two loaves of bread, buy only one, and spend the rest on flowers."

Perspective, how we view ourselves and the world, makes all the difference in what the contours of our life will look like—no matter what the external circumstances turn out to be. So, it is no wonder, then, that a healthy perspective (also known as "enlightenment," "purity of heart," "the secret to a well-lived life") is sought with such dedication by some. And to have such passion is certainly one of the most important prerequisites for finding this pearl of great price. This is so because it enables us to persevere with tenacity—even during the dark days that every one of us must experience as part of being human.

Contemplative and well-known writer Thomas Merton knew this. And so, when he encountered a much older fellow monk who seemed quite depressed and temporarily disconnected from his usual outlook as to what life should be like (what we are calling a "healthy perspective"), he knew what to do and say to him. In response to his companion's lament that he felt he was losing his way, his spirit, his very energy of life, Merton simply responded by gently putting his hand on the sad man's shoulder, smiling at him and advising him (and *us* today when we are going through tough times, I think):

> Brother, courage comes and goes. Hold on for the next supply.

But as we look at such simple wisdom, we see that determination and passion—even with their admittedly great value in the search to gain or regain a healthy perspective—do not represent the total answer. We can have all the energy in the world and be with like-minded searchers but be going very speedily in the *wrong* direction. This is beautifully put forth in the following dialogue between a Zen Master and a would-be disciple. It is a fine and telling example of Buddhist mentorship that can be found reflected in so many similar ways in current psychotherapy and coaching relationships.

> The disciple asks: "Master, how long will it take me to find enlightenment if I enter your community?"
>
> The Master, without hesitating, responds: "Ten years."
>
> The disciple, who is clearly shaken by the time involved, pauses to reflect, looks earnestly up at the Master and pleads, "Well, what if I work really hard?"
>
> "Ah, then," the Master replies, "*twenty* years."

And so, as Clark Strand reminds us in his book *The Wooden Bowl*, removing the blocks to gaining a healthy perspective is a bit like trying to rid oneself of a boomerang. If we have only passion and motivation, we may seek to achieve our goal by trying to throw it away—sometimes with great gusto! But to do so would lead to obvious unsatisfactory results. However, with the right knowledge, we will know when and how to simply set something down in the correct, often gentle, way. Then, like the boomerang we wish to rid ourselves of, we can simply step over it and move on with our lives in a more fruitful way.

POTENT PSYCHOLOGICAL PORTALS TO GAINING A HEALTHIER PERSPECTIVE

From its inception, psychology has also been interested in perspective and saw the value in freeing people from the chains of distorted thinking. In Freud's writings and those of his followers to this day, for example, we see a concern about how we may inadvertently transfer onto the present a way of seeing the world and a resultant style of coping learned in the past—even when the fit is far from perfect. In such instances, according to Freudian thinking, people transfer onto, and live out in, the present what they could not remember from the past. As a result, they have a distorted view of reality and less than satisfactory personal and interpersonal outcomes.

Later on, cognitive-behavioral therapy (CBT) and schema therapy focused on helping people gain greater clarity and a more accurate perception of what was happening. Instead of psychoanalysis and psychodynamic psychotherapy's concern with the past, they are instead interested in the present. They see negative moods as a tip-off that people need to examine their cognitions (ways of perceiving, thinking, and understanding) so they could look further at their underlying beliefs, which are often held without valid support. The goal is to challenge beliefs that are sometimes held with or without clear awareness that prove to be, on closer examination, patently false or, at the very least, somewhat distorted.

Another approach that has now essentially slipped from the center stage of popular psychology is transactional analysis (TA), which was popular in the 1970s. It focuses on helping people to become aware of the games they play, so they can implement changes that result in more fruitful interactions.

And so, if we do value openness and clarity, the obvious question that remains for us to address now—the subject at the heart of this book—is this:

> *What are some of current psychology's most potent portals to gaining, regaining, and maintaining a healthy perspective in order to lead us to deeper personal wisdom and a more meaningful, satisfying, and compassionate life?*

In response to this, in scanning modern clinical psychology's offerings on how to—in practical, concrete ways—improve our sense of reality and acceptance of it, in an effort to make the most of this brief journey we call "life," we find a number of approaches offered that are countercultural and habit-breaking. These include the psychology of "mindfulness," positive psychology and narrative therapy, the modern psychology of gratefulness and happiness, the helpful lessons from studies on posttraumatic *growth*, the psychology of overcoming resistances to openness and change, and techniques in the daily debriefing of self from the schools of cognitive-behavioral therapy and schema therapy as well as the critical thinking and spiritual discernment literature. They are especially important to gaining, regaining, or maintaining a healthy perspective because they encourage us to

- be more nonjudgmental and aware, or psychologically "mindful";
- expand the narrative we have of ourselves or the ones that have been imposed on us;
- understand how to personally debrief ourselves and use structured reflection to see the heretofore unrecognized schemas (beliefs) that may be serving as invisible puppeteers in our lives;
- make "friends" with the resistances to openness so they can atrophy and make room for new possibilities;
- introduce ourselves to the especially helpful aspects of the new psychology of gratefulness and happiness and the ancient wisdom underlying it; and
- see that trauma and the significant stresses that all of us experience need not be the end of the story or the final word, but a source of new meaning making in life.

Seeing these psychological portals to expanding our perspective can be quite a pilgrimage in health and lead to a greater appreciation for so much that is already present, yet so easy to miss, in ourselves and our environment. It would be a shame to avoid the garden of knowledge they provide and ignore the invitation to fathom these portals in today's anxious world. If we are honest, often there is still a hesitancy to see clearly, and act accordingly, as well as to become freer and healthier in how we view our lives and the world around us.

Of such blocks, possibly the main resistance to doing so may be a fear that the work involved in seeking out a healthier perspective is just too hard and time-consuming for us in our already overwrought schedule. Yet, when challenged about all that might be involved in such a pursuit, one mentor retorted with the following simple, challenging question: "How much effort does it take to open your eyes *to see*?"

This question becomes all the more compelling when we start to realize the extent to which the way we view things determines how much more we can enjoy our lives and freely share them with others—*no matter how challenging and dark the circumstances may be!* This is so because a healthy perspective promises so much in realistic immediate terms. In essence:

A Healthy Perspective...

- *Doesn't remove the pain... it limits unnecessary suffering.*
- *Doesn't prevent us from blaming others... it has us withdraw our projections and reclaim our power more quickly.*

- *Doesn't see only what we wish to see... it allows us to better encounter everything that we must face to move forward in life.*
- *Doesn't help us run away from the truth... it enables us to put things in their proper place.*
- *Doesn't eliminate sadness... it allows us to deepen and learn from it.*
- *Doesn't necessarily enable us to be effective when we are compassionate... it helps us to realize that being faithful to reaching out (rather than being successful) is what is truly important.*
- *Doesn't aid us in obtaining more possessions to be happy... it teaches us that real happiness allows us to see all that is there already present in our lives that we are yet to fully enjoy.*
- *Doesn't concern itself so much with the "mental menus" of life's offerings in the future... it aids us to be more present and attentive to exacting the essence out of the real "meals" already set before us.*
- *Doesn't deny the terror of life's traumas... instead it helps us to avoid being permanently crushed as well as to find surprising lessons that might not have been possible to learn had terrible things not happened in the first place.*
- *Doesn't ask us to surrender our intelligence... it encourages us to guard our use of thinking so that emotional and intuitive experiences are valued and examined carefully.*
- *Doesn't solely seek stimulus, novelty, and group experiences... it recognizes the equal importance of periods of solitude, silence, and enjoying the "crumbs of alonetime" available to us.*
- *Doesn't accept our current story or the reputation we may presently have with ourselves... it opens us up to a larger self-narrative that is not determined by society, family, mores, history, or misfortune, but by us.*

- *Doesn't answer all our needs... but instead calls us to re-evaluate and change the way we live by learning what is truly important and meaningful in life.*

And so, in helping us appreciate all of this more readily, we begin to see that being able to gain, regain, or maintain a healthy perspective is, indeed, the pearl of great price.

The real voyage of discovery consists not in seeking new landscapes, but in having new eyes.

MARCEL PROUST, *La Prisonnière*

Psychological Portals to Experiencing a Healthier Perspective

ONE

A Time to See

Creating Space for a More Mindful Life

Is there a quiet stream underneath the fluctuating affirmations and rejections of my little world? Is there a still point where my life is anchored and from which I can reach out with hope and courage and confidence?

Henri J. M. Nouwen, *The Genesee Diary*

Mindfulness is simply about being aware of where your mind is from one moment to the next, with gentle acceptance. This kind of simple attention can have a deeply transformative effect on our daily lives. We can learn to enjoy very ordinary things, such as the flavor of an apple, tolerate great hardship, such as the death of a loved one, just by learning to be aware.

Christopher K. Germer, Ronald D. Siegel, and Paul R. Fulton, *Mindfulness and Psychotherapy*

When a new, healthier perspective is gained, it may be filled with promise that previously wasn't present. At the very least, it can help us to lessen the unnecessary worry and rumination that may be presently dissipating the limited energy at our disposal.

Yet, to be in such a position to gain a broader, healthier perspective, a time for inner stillness is essential—even if it occurs when we are surrounded by people, noise, and the stimulations that seem to sap our spirit and occupy our minds each day. During a lecture trip to Japan, I learned this quite vividly in such a captivating way from a gentle, insightful man.

I had completed delivering a series of lectures in Tokyo and was asked whether I was interested in visiting one of the holiest Shinto shrines in southern Japan: *Ise Jingu.* I was intrigued even more by the possibility of doing this when I heard I would receive a personal tour from a former woodsman who was now the director of the temple grounds. His comments were to be translated for me by someone who spoke both English and Japanese and who had also taught his children.

When my interpreter and I arrived, he met us at the gate and we bowed to each other in traditional Japanese fashion. The tour involved a careful and sensitive explanation of the symbolism and rituals that marked the seasons and life of the tranquil temple grounds and those who visited them.

Amidst this tour and narrative, he led us up to the top of a slightly arched, simply but carefully carved wooden bridge. He then stopped and urged me to look down at the water. When I did, he asked, "What do you see?" After a moment I responded, "Water that is clear, fresh, and at peace." To which he smiled and responded, "*Hai*" (Yes.) Then he looked at me directly with his dark brown eyes, an intent expression on his face, and asked this time, "Now, what do you *hear*?" After another pause, I thought I could make out the sound of a small frog and told him so.

"*Ahso,*" he responded and then with a very serious expression added, "you will not hear *this* species of frog anywhere else on the temple grounds but here." And when I asked why, he quietly but clearly said, "Because this species of frog only lives near water that is clear, fresh, and calm."

I knew enough of the animistic nature of Shintoism to realize that he was not really speaking about frogs and water, but my style of living and the opportunities (or lack of them) that this very style would provide. Would I have periods of silence and possibly solitude to truly experience calm, clarity, and peace, or would I just rush through my life and feel that doing so was "practical," "natural," and "necessary"? After all, doesn't everyone live that way?

Much later, naturalist Peter Matthiessen wrote a similar reflection in a section of his book *Nine-Headed Dragon River*. It made me think back to the above experience and carried the point deeper for me as Matthiessen shared the following comments of spiritual master Yasutani-Roshi

> "The mind of a buddha," Yasutani once said, "is like water that is calm, deep, and crystal clear, and upon which 'the moon of truth' reflects fully and perfectly. The mind of the ordinary man, on the other hand, is like murky water, constantly being churned by the gales of delusive thought and no longer able to reflect the moon of truth. The moon nonetheless shines steadily upon the waves, but as the waters are roiled, we are unable to see its reflection. Thus we

> lead lives that are frustrating and meaningless.... So long as the winds of thought continue to disturb the water of our [real] nature, we cannot distinguish truth from untruth. It is important, therefore, that these winds be stilled. Once they abate, the waves subside, the muddiness clears, and we perceive directly...The moment of such realization is *kensho,* enlightenment...."

Leaning back from the pressures and busyness of life can open the gates to lanes of greater inner freedom not yet traveled. Yet, today most of us leave a number of those potent portals unopened. We may not even know they are there or we may think they are discoverable only by something akin to magic, luck, fame, or winning a major psychological or spiritual lottery (for instance, after finding the "perfect" relationship, career position, or salary, we can *then* be free). But as enticing as our culture advertises these images to be, entertaining them on a continual basis leads us only into emotional and intellectual cul de sacs. Conversely, stepping back in the right way possibly during periods of "alonetime," when in solitude or silently reflecting within oneself, the inner space we need can emerge—not only for our own benefit, but also for the benefit of our family and circle of friends or associates when they turn to us for support. Having a healthy perspective is something we can help "export" through an open presence that encourages freedom borne out of having some quiet time alone. In this sense, it truly enables us to be "the calm within the storm."

Silence, solitude, and mindful moments have the power to stop us in our tracks and ask, why are we continuing to live in such a driven, mindless way? A disconcerting question to us as adults who believe we are already familiar with being responsible people. And, when we say, "We *must* live this way; we have no choice; it is practical and normal so there is really no other way," paradoxically, the *first* gate to new freedom opens to some degree.

This is so because in our hearts, in defending our avoidance of silence and solitude, we already know at some level that what we are telling ourselves is not true. Consequently, once this initial portal of reality is nudged wide a bit, it will never close completely again. And so, this is what the permanent gift of beginning to reflect may offer us, even if we are not fully availing ourselves of such "spaces" yet.

THE CAPACITY TO BE ALONE: RECOGNIZING WE ARE NOT USED TO SILENCE . . . MUCH LESS SOLITUDE!

Silence and solitude—the "places" or "spaces" in which we can take a breath—are surprisingly held suspect in our culture! Thoreau recognized this many years ago and wrote, "If a man walks in the woods for love of them half of each day, he is in danger of being regarded as a loafer. But if he spends his days as a spectator, shearing off those woods and making the earth bald before her time, he is deemed an industrious and enterprising citizen."

Such Thoreau-styled protests, thank goodness, are starting to surface more and more frequently. People increasingly recognize that even intimate relationships, as good and essential as they are, also heavily rely on our having individual quality time alone. Psychologist and spiritual writer Henri Nouwen explains the value of solitude in his book *The Way of the Heart*:

> It is in solitude that this compassionate solidarity grows. In solitude we realize that nothing human is alien to us, that the roots of all conflict, war, injustice, cruelty, hatred, jealousy, and envy are deeply anchored in our own heart. In solitude our heart of stone can be turned into a heart of flesh, a rebellious heart into a contrite heart, and a closed heart into a heart that can open itself to all suffering people in a gesture of solidarity.

Once I was leading a couple of days of recollection on the theme of resilience for Methodist ministers at the New Jersey shore. On the first day I suggested—a bit timidly since they were professional persons of prayer—*they take at least two minutes in silence and solitude and wrapped in gratitude each morning to center themselves before they began their intense day of service to others.* In mentioning only "two minutes," my goal was to encourage regularity—anyone can do two minutes, I thought—as well as to circumvent the usual resistance I experience when suggesting periods of alonetime: "I just don't have time in my busy schedule."

The next morning one of the ministers in the breakfast queue asked whether she might sit with me. "Of course," I said. We gathered our food and sat down together. I smiled at her and asked whether she would like to say grace before our meal, which she did. We then ate slowly, and finally there was a period over coffee when she shared her question: "Do you really take those two minutes each morning that you suggested to us yesterday?" When I told her I really did, she paused, and said, "I tried it this morning. Two minutes seemed like a *long* time!" and we both had to laugh.

Surprisingly, short periods of silence and solitude may not be easy for us—even for those of us in "the mindfulness or prayerfulness business." People who take alonetime seriously know this. In one of his diaries (*A Vow of Conversation*), contemplative Thomas Merton offered the following question and hope that demonstrates the respect all of us should have when we approach quiet time alone. He wrote, "Solitude is a stern master who brooks no nonsense. And the question arises—am I so full of nonsense that she will cast me out? I pray she will not."

Knowing how to be alone is, for the most part, a truly unhonored art that requires both guidance and discipline. Failing to appreciate this can result in self-absorption or moodiness, on the one hand, or a contamination of solitude with an unnecessary myriad of activities or noise within, on the other. Mere silence and solitude may not lead to greater perspective and gratitude. It can lead elsewhere, as was reported by a pastoral leader who had ostensibly dedicated his whole life to finding inner wisdom and being compassionate:

> Someone said to me that these older persons of ministry keep replaying their lives over and over hoping that the ending will be different—and, of course, it never is. I have heard stories of people who make the breakthrough to forgiveness and die soon after and find the peace that sets us free. However, such persons in certain groups—even though they have spent lifetimes in being compassionate caregivers to others—are often rarer than I'd like to say.

THE PSYCHOLOGICAL CAPACITY TO BE ALONE

Psychiatrist Edwin Storr in his seminal work *On Solitude* opened up a discussion among psychotherapists concerning the value of alonetime. In it, he cited the work of therapeutic pioneer Donald Winnicott to make his case on the importance of the capacity to be alone. The following is one of the more intriguing points he made as a part of his argument:

> Winnicott suggests that the capacity to be alone in adult life originates with the infant's experience of being *alone in the presence of the mother*. He is postulating a state in which the

infant's immediate needs for food, warmth, physical contact and so on, have been satisfied, so that there is no need for the infant to be looking to the mother for anything, nor any need for her to be concerned with anything.... I find his conceptions illuminating. He is suggesting that the capacity to be alone originally depends upon what Bowlby would call secure attachment: that is, upon the child being able peacefully to be itself in the presence of the mother without anxiety about her possible departure, and without anxiety as to what may or may not be expected by her.... But Winnicott goes further. He suggests that the capacity to be alone, first in the presence of the mother, and then in her absence, is also related to the individual's capacity to get in touch with, and make manifest, his own true inner feelings. It is only when the child has experienced a contented, relaxed sense of being alone with, and then without, the mother, that he can be sure of being able to discover what he really needs or wants, irrespective of what others may expect or try to foist upon him.

The capacity to be alone thus becomes linked with self-discovery and self-realization; with becoming aware of one's deepest needs, feelings, and impulses.

Storr then goes on to also make a connection of Winnicott's concept regarding the capacity to be alone with the value of meditation. He notes that this version of alonetime facilitates a person's ability to integrate previously unconnected thoughts and feelings by allowing them the time and space to accomplish this valuable objective. He then points out from his vantage point that

> being able to get in touch with one's deepest thoughts and feelings, and providing time for them to regroup themselves into new formations and combinations, are important aspects of the creative process, as well as a way of relieving tension and promoting mental health.
>
> It appears, therefore, that some development of the capacity to be alone is necessary if the brain is to function at its best, and if the individual is to fulfill his highest potential. Human beings easily become alienated from their own deepest needs and feelings. Learning, thinking, innovation, and maintaining contact with one's own inner world are all facilitated by solitude.

WHAT ACTUALLY IS TRUE AWARENESS AND MINDFULNESS?

A sense of mindfulness (being in the present with our eyes wide open) is essentially quite simple. It is the basis of any meditative or informal reflective, centering practice that increases our sense of awareness. Yet, so often as adults we must repeatedly relearn it, no matter how committed we say we are to awareness and appreciation of what is before us. Whereas, mindfulness is actually a state that young children may often appreciate naturally, almost without effort. Jerry Braza, in his book *Moment by*

Moment, notes this in a reflection on his daughter's appreciation of "the awe of the now":

> I recall a time driving my young children somewhere when we approached a railroad crossing as the lights began to flash and the safety gate went down. My first thought was "Oh no! We're going to be held up by a train and be late." Just then, my daughter called out from the backseat, "Daddy, Daddy, we're so lucky! We get to watch the train go by!" Her awareness of the present moment was a wonderful reminder to stop and enjoy what the journey had to offer along the way.

In this story we can see the importance of paying attention to where we are and what we are doing. Often the "now" is filled with many gifts if we have the eyes to see and this can be learned by knowing the basics of mindfulness.

In one of the essays of the edited volume *Mindfulness and Psychotherapy,* Christopher Germer, a leading voice on the psychology of mindfulness, reports and suggests the following with respect to becoming more aware:

> Any exercise that alerts us to the present moment, with acceptance, cultivates mindfulness.... Examples are directing attention to one's breathing, listening to ambient sounds in the environment, paying attention to our posture at a given moment, labeling feelings, and so forth. The list is endless.... Two common exercises for cultivating mindfulness in daily life... involve slowly walking and slow eating.

In his own subsequent authored work *The Mindful Path to Self-Compassion,* Germer also clearly notes what mindfulness is *not* (see Box I). (This is just as important for *us* to note at this point, so take a moment to reflect on his insightful comments to see what your own reactions are to his statements.)

Box I What Mindfulness Is Not

- *Mindfulness is not trying to relax.* When we become aware of what's happening in our lives, it can be anything but relaxing, especially if we're stuck in a difficult situation. As we learn more about ourselves, however, we become less surprised by the feelings that arise within us. We develop a less reactive relationship to inner experience. We can recognize and let go of emotional storms more easily.
- *Mindfulness is not a religion.* Although mindfulness has been practiced by Buddhist nuns and monks for over 2,500 years, any purposeful activity that increases awareness of moment-to-moment experience is a mindfulness exercise. We can practice mindfulness as part of a religion or not. Modern scientific psychology considers mindfulness to be a core healing factor in psychotherapy.
- *Mindfulness is not about transcending ordinary life.* Mindfulness is making intimate contact with each moment of our lives, no matter how trivial or mundane. Simple things can become very special—extraordinarily ordinary—with this type of awareness. For example, the flavor of your food or the color

of a rose will be enhanced if you pay close attention to it. Mindfulness is also about experiencing oneself more fully, not trying to bypass the mundane, ragged edges of our lives.

- *Mindfulness is not emptying the mind of thoughts.* The brain will always produce thoughts—that's what it does. Mindfulness allows us to develop a more harmonious relationship with our thoughts and feelings through a deep understanding of how the mind works. It may *feel* as if we have fewer thoughts because we're not struggling with them so much.
- *Mindfulness is not difficult.* You shouldn't feel disheartened when you discover that your mind wanders incessantly. That's the nature of the mind. It's also the nature of the mind to eventually become aware of its wandering. Ironically, it's in the very moment when you despair that you're not mindful that you've become mindful. It's not possible to do this practice perfectly, nor is it possible to fail. That is why it's called a "practice."
- *Mindfulness is not escape from pain.* This is the toughest idea to accept because we rarely do anything without the wish to feel better. You *will* feel better with mindfulness and acceptance, but only by learning *not* to escape from pain. Pain is like an angry bull: When it's confined to a tight stall, it will be wild and try to escape. When it's in a wide-open field, it will calm down. Mindfulness makes emotional space for pain.

Source: C. Germer, *The Mindful Path to Self-Compassion* (New York: Guilford Press, 2009). Used with permission.

PAYING ATTENTION DIFFERENTLY IN SOLITUDE

Being alone may mean many different things to different people. For some it may be a chance to do mindless activity. For others, though, whether they are straightening items in a closet or planting a row of tulips, the activity or time sitting quietly is mindfully spent.

Mindfulness allows life to come up before us without judgment during periods of silence or solitude. It has us leave nothing out, while not indulging anything either negatively or positively. In a spirit of mindfulness, we observe, experience, and learn. The process simply involves watching, breathing, and living in the now—ideally with a sense of wonder. Perhaps it is not so "simple." And so, writers and mentors of mindfulness offer guidance on how to keep the process as elementary as an unpolished stone. Included in such guidance is a need for us to remember that mindfulness

- embraces that everything is fresh each time: expectations—even if they are based on how something originally happened in the past—defeat this;
- doesn't lead to regret and encourages us to return to the now when *mindlessness* gets us trapped in the past or preoccupied with the future;
- is about that which is real—not the ideal, and not positive or negative fantasies or concepts;

- accepts that everything—*every* thing—changes;
- encourages us to see—honestly and completely—how every action and comment has an impact on others in our interpersonal network, and to some degree on ourselves; and
- appreciates the specific impacts of word and actions taken, not general philosophies.

And so, with a sense of *awareness* (or what most refer to as "mindfulness"), we appreciate that the openness we truly embrace can make all the difference in how we perceive and value a life of truth, presence, and being awake—and, in turn, how it makes itself known in the many different facets of life.

Mindfulness ensures that we are awake. It also sets the stage for important learning during the difficult times in life "*if* only we have the eyes to see." We have a healthy perspective—no matter what is going on in our lives at any given time. On the other hand, "mind*less*ness" not only keeps us blind to all that we should be grateful for, but it also prevents us from being all that we can truly be (see Box 2).

Box 2 The Red Flags of Mindlessness

When we live without a sense of mindfulness, we miss and waste a good deal of energy. However, when we are able to recognize those red flags that indicate when we are not really experiencing awareness of what is happening within and

Box 2 (Continued)

around us, we can more quickly and mindfully return to "the now" with a sense of openness. Therefore, it is helpful to recognize and acknowledge some red flags of mindlessness:

- We get easily upset—often over the wrong things—and miss what life is offering us in all interactions and events.
- Interruptions are seen only as disruptive rather than informative or possible, unexpected opportunities.
- Habits and rules continue to sap life's freshness from us.
- We spend too much time in the silver casket of nostalgia or rushing through precious moments of our lives under the impression that living this way is "only practical."
- We only fantasize about "the spirit of simplicity" and "letting go" rather than seeking to practice them more in our lives.
- Our promise to ourselves to adopt a healthier lifestyle doesn't translate into the necessary actions.
- We spend so much of the time in a cognitive cocoon of judgment, worry, preoccupation, resentment, fear, and regret that we miss life's daily gifts happening all around us.
- Our time in silence and solitude often ends up being boring and emotionally flat rather than renewing.
- We seem to ignore the spiritual gifts of laughter, a child's smile, or a good conversation and instead focus on increasing such trivial things as fame, power, security, and pleasure.

- A cancelled get-together, a brief illness, or a delay in our schedule is not appreciated as a spontaneous period for spiritual mindfulness.
- Transitions make up much of our life but are not seen as being as valuable as our destinations.
- The "ghosts" of our past memories are not valued as the teachers they can be, but instead merely serve to pull us down or fill us with regret.
- A sense of intrigue or curiosity about ourselves—including both our gifts and growing edges (those areas which we are defensive about or need further development)—is overshadowed by our self-blame, discouragement, or projecting faults onto others.
- Too much of our lives is spent running away from what we don't like or in "medicating" ourselves, seeking security, or grasping, rather than simply enjoying and being grateful for all that is around us.
- Sincerity, transparency, and being a person without guile seems absent even though we know we waste so much unnecessary energy on being defensive, wearing masks to obscure our true selves, or seeking to manipulate others.
- We rush around like a gargoyle on roller skates while failing to notice people we have hurt, what we are eating, how we are feeling, what we are really doing, or to where we should be directing our attention (such as the road when we are driving a car or the person to whom we are speaking).

And so, as part of our journey to become more awake (so we can perceive more accurately what is going on in and around us), we must be able to pick up and attend to the unique characteristics of mindfulness, such as the following:

- A clear awareness of what we are experiencing, thinking, or feeling without judging ourselves or others
- A sense of intrigue about ourselves and others without projection (blaming others), self-condemnation, discouragement, or expectations
- Increased interest in discovering the gifts of life rather than merely focusing on our accomplishments
- An appreciation of being in the now and a willingness to return to the present when we are drawn into the past or begin to be preoccupied by the future
- A spirit of "unlearning" and a willingness to see life differently that is inspired by the call to "make all things new"
- A non-ego-centered approach to life that recognizes that "it isn't all about *me*"
- A willingness to recognize, embrace, and flow with change
- A spirit of receiving life as it is, without reaction or rejection
- Appreciation of the beauty of patience, which allows us to enjoy the process of life rather than solely looking forward to completions or successes
- An interest in letting go of the "training" we have received in grasping or being envious, angry, and unkind; and instead having an openness to: sharing without an expectation of

getting anything in return; being intrigued by our responses so we can learn from them rather than responding in self-defense or self-indictment; and slowing down rather than straining toward goals (even perceived good ones)

- Avoidance of comparing ourselves favorably or unfavorably with others
- A greater desire to be sensitive to how our words and actions affect others
- An interest in seeking—even in little ways—to contribute to well-being rather than suffering for others and ourselves
- Openness to "mindfully touching" all of our denials, loneliness, shame, and negative feelings about ourselves with compassion rather than running away from them
- Allowing information, negative and positive, familiar and unfamiliar, to flow to us without being obstructed or modified by our ego or fears
- An increased desire for transparency and authenticity in the way we live so we can help purify—rather than contaminate with our defensiveness—the psychological and spiritual atmosphere in which we and others live

Practicing, not simply knowing *about*, these characteristics of mindfulness may result in our being more open to receive all that life might offer. In addition, and of possibly even more import, doing this will help us face life's difficulties, gray periods, or sad experiences and deepen us in ways we may never have dreamed possible, which will also be a gift to those around us.

RELEASING PREVIOUSLY UNACCOUNTED-FOR ENERGY

Whether we recognize it or not, we spend much of the day in front of a mental mirror whose distortions are dramatic because of the positive and negative characteristics attributed to us by the people with whom we interact. This is so because of *their* personal needs and personality styles. These distortions from the outside may also trigger in some cases our own long-standing (characterological) inner and situational blind spots. Fortunately, meditation and clearer awareness can raise these blind spots and cognitive distortions up to the surface of our consciousness, especially when we have a gentle, clear mentor with whom to process them. When this happens, all we need do is not close our "perceptual eyes." Yet, psychologically, often without knowing it, we, at the very least, "squint."

In his book *A Path with Heart*, psychologist and Buddhist dharma teacher Jack Kornfield, recognizing this tendency, recalls the guidance of his teacher, Achaan Chah, who said that in meditation, metaphorically, "Just go into the room and put one chair in the center. Take the one seat in the center of the room, open the doors and windows, and see who comes to visit. You will witness all kinds of scenes and actors, all kinds of temptations and stories, everything imaginable. Your only job is to stay in your seat. You will see it all arise and pass, and out of this, wisdom and understanding will come."

In doing this, Kornfield suggests we create space in ourselves that allows memories and emotions to rise and teach us where our unaccounted-for energy—hidden in unrecognized sadness and shame, resentment and regret, desire and loneliness, and even happiness and joy—may lie. We are also given the opportunity to experience how mindfulness can help guide us to a place where we can possess a healthier perspective (see Box 3).

Box 3 The Fruits of Mindfulness and a Healthy Perspective

When we are suffering or our lives seem "dark," mindfulness helps us to be more in tune with what life has to teach us, sometimes in new, transforming ways. When we are in "the now" and open, mindfulness can help us in the following ways:

- Lift us out of stagnant, obsessive thought patterns
- Alert us to when we are not living the experience of life but merely wandering around in an envelope of thought, thinking we are alive
- Move us out of the thicket of preoccupations, fears, anxieties, and worries about the past or future by having us "simply" be where we are

(*continued*)

Box 3 (Continued)

- Help us appreciate that *all* things/people/situations change
- Give us the space to step back and get unglued from our desires, demands, and attachments so we can have the freedom to flow with what is
- Enable us to get in touch with the invisible bonds of shame, loneliness, secrets, addictions, hopes, and other places in our hearts where we have expended a great deal of energy in avoidance
- Help us forgo the comfort of denial and avoidance for the peace that allows us to fear nothing but instead welcome all of our emotions, cognitions (ways of thinking, perceiving, and understanding), and impulses with compassion and clarity
- Open up true space for others by opening it up in ourselves
- Help us imitate Buddha, Jesus, and others we admire by reaching out to others who are in need
- Enable us to see our defenses, failures, and growing edges as opportunities for new wisdom and opening to life (because rather than judging, we are intrigued by them)
- Ask us if we are relating to ourselves with kindness and clarity
- Awaken us to our habitual, possibly deadening styles of thinking, believing, and behaving
- Allow us especially to become freer by taking "the sacred pause" spiritual guide Tara Brach suggests when confronted with suffering (this pause is made up of a desire to

recognize what is happening, allowing it, and experiencing it rather than trying to just figure out or control it)

- Help us see that permanent problems are so because of the way we formulate them, thus teaching us that loosening our grip on such ways of seeing our world makes all the difference
- Set aside the way we have created meaning so all things can be made new
- Increase our appreciation of how little things can produce emotional peaks and valleys in our lives
- Develop our respect for both formal mindfulness (meditation) and informal approaches to mindfulness that will increase our awareness of "the now" during the day
- Incorporate simple practices, such as taking a few moments to notice something enjoyable; appreciating our own small, beautiful acts; and slowing down when we are caught up in a sense of mindless, driven action
- Encourage us to wonder more about what thoughts, emotions, and events help us create peace rather than suffering
- Teach us that being spiritually aware is more natural when we don't seek it aggressively, or with expectations or fear that it won't produce dramatic results
- Have us welcome and learn from, rather than label and reject, so-called negative experiences such as boredom
- Help us be clear and sort things out as well as deepen ourselves
- Encourage humility, help us see our foibles, and over time increase the enjoyment we have in being alone with ourselves and relaxed with others

(*continued*)

Box 3 (Continued)

- Become less dependent on reinforcement by others while at the same time setting the stage for taking a healthier part in community
- Protect our inner fire by helping us see when we need to withdraw for time alone and also uncover time within our daily activity in which we can take a few breaths and center ourselves, rather than be disturbed that we are being delayed or postponed in our travels or activities
- Make us more in tune with the inner voice of a healthy perspective that is continually being drowned out by society and our own inner habitual self-talk

CREATING FAMILIAR PLACES OF SOLITUDE

One of the most practical steps to encourage mindfulness meditation as a part of our daily life is to have familiar places in which to experience it. Yet, such places in the world seem so limited today that we must take extra steps to discover them. In Sara Maitland's words,

> Silence, even as an expression of awe, is becoming uncomfortable. We are asked to be silent less and less; churches and

> public libraries are no longer regarded as places where silence is appropriate....[S]ilence is not experienced as refreshing or as assisting concentration, but as threatening and disturbing....Nonetheless, despite the rising tide of noise, there are some real pools of silence embedded in the noisiest places and I began to search them out.

She reflects further in *A Book of Silence* on how important silence and solitude are, particularly for a writer. When she moved to a house far away from everything, a friend of hers reacted strongly, which I think tells us once again that people's views of alonetime differ quite markedly:

> Virginia Woolf famously taught us that every woman writer needs a room of her own. She didn't know the half of it, in my opinion. I need a moor of my own. Or, as an exasperated but obviously sensitive friend commented when she came to see my latest lunacy, "Only you, Sara—twenty mile views of absolutely nothing!"
>
> It isn't "nothing," actually—it is cloud formations, and the different ways reed, rough grass, heather and bracken move in the wind, and the changing colours, not just through the year but through the day as the sun and the clouds alternate and shift...and it is the huge nothing that pulls me into itself. I looked at it, and with fewer things to look at I see better....I can see occasional, and apparently unrelated, strips of silver, which are in fact the small river meandering down the valley....I think about how beautiful it is, and how happy I am.

Henry David Thoreau, one of our leading muses of silence and solitude, felt he could not preserve his health and spirit if he did not spend a significant amount of time sauntering "through the woods and over the hills and fields absolutely free from worldly engagements." We may not have as much time as Thoreau did to devote to such endeavors. In addition, we may not wish to find ourselves in a rural or woodland setting. As a matter of fact, sometimes we may think of solitude as a back-to-nature movement that Thoreau, and later Maitland, seemed to be suggesting. However, this needn't be the case.

Hugh Prather, for instance, humorously notes that "what is conducive to concentration for one person is not for another. Solitude is often associated with the fact of getting away from people, and into nature, but my wife Gayle, for example, is more at rest in a large city than in the wilderness. 'Nature makes you itch,' she says. She's convinced that camping out invites angry bears and ax murderers. And certainly it makes no sense to say that in order to feel what connects us all, we must always get away from each other."

However, with an appreciation of mindful silence, our time—however long or wherever it may be—can still have a significant influence on us for the better. In her book *Contentment: Wisdom from Around the World,* Gillian Stokes notes, "You do not have to live in a cave on a mountaintop to realize spiritual contentment, but if you have become habituated to noise and bustle, you might find it easier to reach a sense of contentment in a less hectic environment, at least in the beginning." The goal is not to run away but to find those spaces that are conducive to us—even in, *especially* during, times of difficulty.

As Viktor Frankl, Holocaust survivor and author of *Man's Search for Meaning,* aptly noted, "To live you must choose; to love you must encounter; to grow you must suffer." Yet this doesn't happen spontaneously. Such growth during times of sadness needs to be fed by a sense of informal mindfulness as well as—whenever possible—its formal counterpart (meditation).

A graduate course that I led dealt to a great extent with such an interest in these forms of awareness. One of the participants addressed the reasons of how and why she was drawn to a spirit of reflection, meditation, and being in the present moment. She clearly heard this message and took it to heart:

> I so well remember a few years ago when I was invited to a Buddhist place of meditation in Washington, DC. There was a week-long retreat taking place, and my friend and I were allowed to join them for a few hours of sitting and walking meditation that day. I then had the unexpected opportunity to have a few moments to speak privately with the Vietnamese monk who was leading the retreat. I asked him quite bluntly: "Why do you meditate?" He answered in his almost perfect English, "I meditate to be happy. When I am in the present moment, I am happy. If I think on the past, then I am often sorry. If I think about the future, I often worry. So then I am often sorry, worry, sorry, worry, sorry, worry. But when I meditate I am in the present, and I am happy."

> The simplicity and accuracy of this simple explanation struck a deep chord in me, and I have related this story many times to friends. I am all too familiar with the "sorry-worry" obsession that plays in my head all too often. Author Eckhart Tolle expresses it so well when he writes: "Stress is caused by being 'here' but wanting to be 'there' or being in the present but wanting to be in the future. It is a split that tears you apart inside." This is one reason that meditation is a lifeline for me. It is a time for me to quietly remember to be present and, hopefully, it will spill over into the rest of my day.

No doubt we would want the same to be said of our commitment to having mindfulness meditation at the core of our lives. Yet, for this to be so, we must not only have the motivation, we must also employ the basic approaches to meditating in silence and solitude that have been passed down through the ages. Psychologist and spiritual writer Jack Kornfield once said that you wouldn't go hiking in the Himalayas without a guide, so why would you want to travel the even more demanding travails of the inner life without the guidance that is available?

This is particularly sensible for us to consider since we have some simple wisdom on mindfulness that our predecessors have left us to both reflect upon and use. Our only response to having such guidance must be a threefold process: understand it, absorb it, and, more important, *use* it. Yet, to do so, we need to have the time and space to allow for such a practice.

TIME AND SPACE TO BE MINDFUL

George Prochnik, in his recent popular work *In Pursuit of Silence: Listening for Meaning in a World of Noise,* reflects on time and space: "We probably do not need a pervasive silence—desirable as this might seem to some. What we do need is more space in which we can interrupt our general experience of noise. What we must aspire to is a greater proportion of quiet in the course of everyday life."

He then points out a financial limitation for many about taking significant periods of silence:

> I cherish the memory of the time I spent on a silent retreat at an ashram, gazing at a group of people scattered across a grassing hillside like roosting birds—all of them concentrated on doing nothing but being still and listening to the natural world. But the people who go to ashrams, vipassana centers, and all the rich variants of silent-meditation retreats are, for the most part, reasonably well off. Like me, they had the money, the time, or simply the social context that enabled them to wake up one day and say to themselves, "You know what? I'm going on a silent retreat." I'm worried about all the people who, for one reason or another, lack the resources to discover what silence can bring.

Still, keep in mind that there are places that all of us can access if we really look carefully for them. They include places of worship in our large cities that are open during the day—possibly between services. Libraries; small, urban gardens or large parks; walkways along rivers and streams; and little coffee-houses during the off hours are but a few that quickly come to mind. We need to be aware of locations that could "double" as a place of refuge rather than simply dismissing the possibilities, saying, "I can't do it. There is no place available for me."

We also need to create a conducive place for ourselves in our homes and offices so that when the opportunity spontaneously presents itself or we have initiated a ritual of silence during our day (perhaps morning meditation or quiet evening reflection), we know where we will do it.

For some, it may be a corner of a room or a separate place. It need not be fancy, just enhancing to the process of silence and solitude. Richard Hauser, Jesuit priest and author of works on Christian spirituality, describes his quiet space for prayer that can be used by everyone for meditation:

> I pray in my own room—which doubles as a bedroom—in a chair next to a large window with an eastward exposure, overlooking a secluded garden…; the chair faces my prayer wall. It is upholstered and comfortable, but supports me firmly in an upright position. Alongside the chair on a side table I place all the materials I need.… I love this room; it is away from my offices. The window, open in warm weather, gives direct access to the sights and sounds of the garden and to the warmth and light of the rising sun. My prayer

wall is hung with favorite icons, [and] prints...gathered over the years; I rearrange the wall for different liturgical seasons and feasts. The physical setting—the time, place, furniture arrangement—is key....Prayer can be simple: just find the right time and place and go there regularly!

SIMPLE APPROACHES TO FORMAL MINDFULNESS MEDITATION

Once we have addressed the issue of *where* (conducive places), the question of *how* comes to mind. And, as well as improving our sense of nonjudgmental mindfulness/awareness in general, we must simultaneously attend to our formal meditation practice. And so, for those who are unfamiliar with meditation practice, I offer the following simple suggestions to foster a beginning practice. (For further reading, see the recommended books on the topic listed at the end of this book; a mentor or guide will help develop and deepen your practice.)

- *Maintain a posture that is conducive.* As we sit, with our back straight, we look just ahead at something to hold our attention (e.g., a candle) as we breathe naturally and gently.
- *Be patient.* Rushing or expecting something only injects unnecessary pressure into our time of meditation. Be the apple slowly ripening.

- *Don't unduly entertain, judge, or run away from your thoughts.* Just observe and let them move through you like water in a slowly running stream. To help accomplish this, you can label thoughts (e.g., "judging," "guilt") that come your way, or use a centering word/mantra like "gentle," or even count your breaths from 1 to 4, and keep counting this way until you are present again.
- *Accept where you are in meditation, and don't compare.* After all, what choice do you have than to be where you are at this point? Also, don't waste time in favorably or unfavorably comparing your meditation, or anything about yourself, with others. Meditation is not a competition or beauty pageant.
- *Don't seek to solve anything in meditation.* Problem-solving is a good activity but not appropriate to formal mindfulness.
- *Don't expect or try to force anything.* Just relax; that's enough. Trust. The meditation will do the rest. There will be times when we are meditating that it will flow easily. Other times our meditation may seem flat, empty. We may even be bored for a time. That is all right. As Zen teaches us, if you are bored for two minutes in meditation, then do it for four!
- *Don't cling.* Just breathe in good energy and breathe out peace; then let whatever comes up flow through you like a light wind. If some issue or theme repeatedly surfaces, just come back to your centering word or counting your breaths from 1 to 4 again and again until you are settled. Breathing in and out is an anchor in meditation and allows the practice to ebb and flow naturally.

- *Although you should have a regular meditation practice, make time for intense, longer meditative periods.* Taking at least a few moments each day to center yourself is essential, and cultivating discipline to meditate regularly is the spiritual backbone of a life well lived. However, if possible, extend your meditation sessions for longer periods of time.

INCLUDING EVERYTHING

One of the most important elements of mindfulness meditation as an aid to maintaining or regaining a healthy perspective is to include everything in the practice of it. Jack Kornfield, once again in his Eastern spirituality work *A Path with Heart,* notes,

> I had hoped for special effects from meditation—happiness, special states of rapture, extraordinary experiences. But that was not primarily what my teacher offered. He offered a way of life, a lifelong path of awakening, attention, surrender, and commitment. He offered a happiness that was not dependent on any of the changing conditions of the world but came out of one's own difficult and conscious inner transformation. In joining the monastery, I had hoped to leave behind the pain of my family life and the difficulties of the world, but of course they followed me. It took many years for me to realize that these difficulties were part of my practice.... The simple phrase, "This too, this too," was the main meditation

instruction of [another of the spiritual masters] with whom I studied. Through these few words we were encouraged to soften and be open to see whatever we encountered, accepting the truth with a wise and understanding heart.

What enriches mindfulness is including all of the *specifics* of life. When something joyful, puzzling, sad, or upsetting happens—no matter how inconsequential it seems at first—we must remember to bring "this too, this too" to our meditation and mindfulness. Viewing even our distractions as sources of new knowledge is a response that will reap great rewards. The goal of this approach is to transform our entire life into a rich, mindful one. In this way, rather than being tied down by so many other "voices" (culture, peer pressure, family fears, neediness, etc.), we can respond to the truth's sometimes soft inner voice that calls us to the new freedom and fuller life that a healthy perspective can foster.

GOING ON RETREAT: PERIODS OF DRAMATIC SOLITUDE

Philosopher Henry David Thoreau, as was previously noted, is probably one of the best-known solitude-seeking Americans. His reasons for seeking solitude remain compelling today:

> I went to the woods because I wished to live deliberately, to front only the essential facts of life, and see if I could

> not learn what it had to teach, and not, when I came to die, discover that I had not lived. I did not wish to live what was not life, living is so dear; nor did I wish to practice resignation, unless it was quite necessary. I wanted to live deep and suck out all the marrow of life, to live so sturdily and Spartan-like as to put to rout all that was not life, to cut a broad swath and shave close, to drive life into a corner, and reduce it to its lowest terms, and, if it proved to be mean, why then to get the whole and genuine meanness of it, and publish its meanness to the world; or if it were sublime, to know it by experience, and be able to give a true account of it in my next excursion.

More dramatic than Thoreau's retreat to the woods is the one described in *A Woman in the Polar Night* by Christiane Ritter. In the introduction, Lawrence Millman writes,

> Stuck in the hut by herself during an epic snowstorm, Christiane almost did go crazy. At the same time, she realized that, however tough the circumstances, she could survive them. And from then on, she did not think of the Arctic as an enemy. Rather, it was a realm "where everything goes its prescribed way ... without man's intervention." Such was her transformation that she could even suggest that "in centuries to come, men will go to the Arctic as in biblical times they withdrew to the desert, to find the truth again." I can't imagine any polar explorer making a statement like this....

> Christiane left what she called "the Arctic wilderness" in June of 1935, never to return....[S]he didn't really need to return...since she brought it home with her, or at least brought home a radically different way of looking at the world. A short while after she got back from Spitsbergen, the Ritter family estate burned to the ground. But rather than go into mourning over the loss of her home and virtually all of her possessions, Christiane was more or less grateful, according to her daughter Karin. For she could now live simply, without a surfeit of ballast, just as she lived in the hut in Grahuken.

Ritter's account of living in a very small hut alone for protracted periods of time is interesting to read because she vividly captures her experiences and the lessons she learned. She became filled with the gratitude that can come only after one has felt deprivation; one feels new appreciation of what is often taken for granted.

Much less dramatic than these accounts, though, are the reflections of people who go on a silent retreat by themselves or with others who will also respect the need to move away from noise and even good conversation for a while. Such a period may be for 30 days, a week, or, as is a more likely scenario for most of us, an overnight or weekend experience. After taking such time, many of the people I have interviewed report a combination of—in their own interpretation—pleasant and disagreeable experiences:

- "I recognized how much was swirling around in my mind just below the surface."

- "I had forgotten what the simple truth really is because even conversations within myself often sounded like cocktail party discussions."
- "I realized I rarely challenged my shame but covered it over with intellectualizations"
- "I crossed those boundaries with someone I work with at the restaurant because she needed extra physical assurance of my interest in her."
- "There were fears in me that if I saw how I needed to change and did it, others would shy away from me. I would see how I had not really lived up to this point in my life, or if I did see the truth I would have to do something about it."

All told, people who retreated from society gained knowledge that was informative and beneficial in ways that would not have been possible had they taken a shorter period of solitude, such as a few hours or a day that most of us allow ourselves (see Box 4).

Box 4 Illustrations of Positive Movements Toward Mindfulness in Our Lives

- We begin to see peace, joy, understanding, and patience spontaneously take the place of anger, resentment, and other negative emotions.
- When someone misbehaves rather than merely react, we reflect and act in a helpful way.

Box 4 (Continued)

- We frequently replace judging ourselves or others with a helpful compassion that can lead to positive change.
- We suffer less crippling guilt, which pulls us into the past and leaves us there; we become aware of our faults, but in a way that makes the present and future different.
- We recognize when we have become inordinately preoccupied with the future, and we develop a greater appreciation of the present moment and the ability to stay in that moment.
- We cultivate a more natural tendency to move away from useless worry. In its place we meet life's demands more often with a concern that involves recognizing the challenges, appreciating their source, planning what we can do, doing it, and then letting it lie.
- We view ourselves and those around us with acceptance, compassion, and understanding.
- We cultivate a deeper appreciation for patience and vulnerability instead of a desire to control.
- We more readily experience surprising episodes of gratitude for people and things we used to take for granted in our daily encounters.
- We become less interested in competition, less concerned about what others may think of us.

- We experience collaboration and connectedness spontaneously.
- We feel a real sense of intrigue about our own thoughts, ways of understanding, perceptions, emotions, and behaviors rather than the old tendency toward self-blame, resentment, or fear.
- We don't automatically believe our thoughts—especially the negative ones—without checking them out.
- Our self-awareness becomes more a gentle process of self-appreciation rather than a process of comparison between ourselves and others.
- We seek to be more inclusive rather than exclusive in the way we bring everything into our meditation and lives.
- We desire to use our speech to benefit others by being truthful, expressive of our own experiences, sensitive to the feelings of others, supportive, encouraging, accurate, and specific rather than vague, negative, and self-referential in an exaggerated way.

When we experience these positive movements in mindfulness meditation, we discover why and how making alonetime part of our entire day, not just part of our formal meditation, results in a more centered, full, and compassionate way of life. Surely, aspiring to live in such a wonderful way is a noble and rewarding goal.

Alonetime, like anger and most other encounters or reactions, is not beneficial in and of itself. It is our approach to, and perception of, this time that makes all the difference. That is why the information on informal and formal mindfulness (meditation) that helps us to lean back from both our busy schedules and cluttered minds filled with thoughts and judgments is so necessary. It is also essential to recognize the natural resistances we have to spending time alone so we can continue to enhance our alonetime rather than succumb to our blocks to it. To conclude here, in the words of the poet Rilke,

> For what (ask yourself) would solitude be that had no greatness; there is but *one* solitude, and that is great, and not easy to bear, and to almost everybody come hours when they would gladly exchange it for any sort of intercourse, however banal and cheap, for the semblance of some slight accord with the first comer, with the unworthiest.... But perhaps those are the very hours when solitude grows.... But that must not mislead you. The necessary thing is after all but this: solitude, great inner solitude. Going-into-oneself and for hours meeting no one—this one must be able to attain. To be solitary, the way one was solitary as a child, when the grownups went around involved with things that seemed important and big because they themselves looked so busy and because one comprehended nothing of their doings.... And you should not let yourself be confused in

your solitude by the fact that there is something in you that wants to break out of it. This very wish will help you, if you use it quietly, and deliberately and like a tool, to spread out your solitude over wide country.

SOME QUESTIONS TO CONSIDER AT THIS POINT

Where in your life does quiet time already exist? [1]

In what parts of your life is it realistic to create some new spaces where you can relax and practice mindful breathing?

Imagine people in your life that you admire because they are more reflective and relaxed than you are. What are some basic ways to emulate them?

In what ways can you create an environment in your home or office that is conducive to taking a brief period for sitting quietly and reflecting or meditating?

How can you develop a list of triggers to help you become more mindful so you don't simply run to your grave thinking that once this one task, job, or thing is done you will take time? (These reminders can and should include common daily triggers such as the ring or vibration of a cellphone,

[1] At the end of most chapters, questions will be provided to assist in personalizing the material just presented. As such, reflective time with responses to these questions can have as much—if not greater—impact than the information just read on setting the stage for developing a more consistently healthy perspective.

unlocking your car to drive to work or on an errand, your morning alarm.)

In your own life, how would you describe the relationship between alonetime and the relationships you have at work and in your personal life?

What has been your own array of experiences when you took time in silence and possibly solitude?

If you have a formal mindfulness meditative practice, how do you handle distractions during meditation?

What unique characteristics of mindfulness have you experienced, and which ones noted in this chapter have you not?

What are you favorite places of solitude?

What are the most important approaches to meditation for you?

If you use a diary to note your reflections after meditation or periods of alonetime, in what ways has this practice been helpful for you?

If you don't record your impressions, do you think you might like to begin? What would it take for you to do this?

TWO

Seeing Ourselves More Completely

Fathoming the Lessons of Positive Psychology and Narrative Therapy

"Why is everyone here so happy except me?"
"Because they have learned to see goodness and beauty everywhere," Said the Master.
"Why don't I see goodness and beauty everywhere?"
"Because you cannot see outside of you what you fail to see inside."

Anthony de Mello, *One Minute Wisdom*

So, as long as you are trying to be something other than what you actually are, your mind merely wears itself out.

Krishnamurti, *Life Ahead*

A colleague of mine accepted a position in Egypt for a brief assignment. During this period, his work took him across the city of Cairo every day on a three-car trolley. Although the streetcars all appeared to be quite the same, one was designated as "first class" and charged a slightly higher fare. Intrigued by this, he finally mustered the courage to ask a fellow passenger what made the difference. After a protracted pause, the co-traveler said, "It is true that the cars are the same, but the difference between first and second class is *what you think of yourself*."

Sitting across from people requesting therapy, mentoring, or simply a word of support, I have more often than not had a strange intuitive feeling that often proved to be true: even though we had just met, I seemed to think more of them than they did of themselves. This awareness was spurred by my early experiences as a clinician. During a simple interchange in supervision, I was taught to look at my patients and people differently, more holistically, by eminent Philadelphia psychiatrist Franklin West.

Following one of my case presentations, he said, "Bob, you have done an excellent job of clarifying the issues your patient is facing as well as uncovering and highlighting his psychological defenses and psychopathology. However, you have not put enough energy in also bringing into sharp focus his talents, gifts, and strengths. And so, the picture is not balanced. Moreover, if he has only problems and no positive strengths, then that means you will have to do all the pulling since he has nothing to work with." I have never forgotten this lesson, and it repeatedly came back to me with the dawning of such therapeutic schools as cognitive-behavioral therapy, positive psychology, and narrative therapy—and in a particularly marked way years later with one of my patients.

One of the nicest settings that I ever had for my clinical practice was in Marriottsville, Maryland. My office was in a spirituality center surrounded by 128 acres of fields and woodlands. Once, a peahen took up residence near a bush just outside my office. Another time, for several days, a fawn lay under my window.

Given the presence of majestic oaks and mature spruces, the center was especially breathtaking in the snow. So the first snowstorm of the season was quite an event to celebrate, and one winter it arrived when I was there to see patients. I looked up and absorbed the beauty as it coated the landscape; I smiled and thought, "Wow."

Immediately following that experience, I got caught up in the back-to-back sessions of the day and looked out again when it was early afternoon, and the snow had started to really mount up. When I saw it all, the previous poetic appreciation of the landscape immediately disappeared. Now I thought, "Oh no! How am I ever going to get out of here when the day is over?" (Obviously my spiritual appreciation of nature was not too consistent.)

Just as I was thinking this, the phone rang. It was a patient who was also a psychologist. She said, "I am not coming in today." Still annoyed about the weather, I said, "Well, it is up to *you*." She could hear something in the tone of my voice and said, "Well, you are not going to charge me for the missed session are you?" I replied, a bit irked by the question, "Well, you know you need to give twenty-four hours' notice if you don't wish to be charged."

You could tell by the sharp intake of her breath that she was shocked and annoyed as she responded, "Well, then, I'm coming in!" and she abruptly hung up before I could say anything. As I sat there I thought, "Oh, no. Under the circumstances, I would now willingly pay her *not* to come in."

When she finally arrived, she surprised me. Rather than displaying anger, she showed something totally different. She was smiling. After taking it in, I asked, "How come you are smiling? I thought you would be furious at me for the foolish way I responded over the phone."

She continued smiling and replied quite simply, "*You* were angry."

To which I replied, "No I wasn't."

She looked at me puzzled and said, "You weren't?"

"No, to be honest, I was *furious*. You caught me when I was in a real mood about the weather. But I still don't know why you are smiling rather than angry."

"Well, when you were angry at me, I experienced the *real* you."

After a pause that allowed me to take in what she was saying, I saw her reaction to my immature behavior as a chance to use the situation to her advantage. I pointed out a disparity that was important for her to recognize about her own self-image and said, "It seems to me that in the past when I have given you positive feedback, it didn't seem as real to you. However, when I behaved poorly and reacted in a negative way earlier today, for some reason this seemed more real to you. Why do you think you hear positive feedback in a whisper and negative reactions as thunder?"

It is important for us to have an accurate self-image so we don't dismiss the positive feedback we receive or miss the signature strengths we have. If we view ourselves in a balanced way, we can be freer and more integrated. Moreover, given the presence of our talents, in turn, we are in a stronger position to be compassionate to many different types of people, no matter how they react to us. This will save psychic energy instead of wasting it on trying to develop several personalities or feeling we must don different defensive masks depending on our company. Seeing our gifts more clearly will also help us to develop more fully as persons because we will be able to tend to them and share them more effectively with others.

In addition, it will help us to better monitor the meaning or messages we give ourselves all day. This is referred to as "self-talk" in psychology, or what I prefer to call quiet "self-whispers," since they often go unrecognized and therefore remain unexamined or unchallenged. With a real sense of self we can approach situations with a greater sense of certainty and humility. Consequently, rather than feeling we need to always seek approval or reinforcement (though some is natural and good), we can act out of our true identity. If positive results occur, fine; if negative ones occur, well, fine too, because—with a healthy perspective—they will teach us something.

When we feel ourselves becoming anxious, depressed, or stressed, we can ask questions that will get us back in touch with our true calling. This will help us to see that our fears and "dis-ease" are arising out of playing a role, fearing rejection, or being revealed as a charlatan of some type. To help us counter this, some questions we need to ask ourselves when having negative feelings include the following:

- Why am I making myself so anxious or angry in this situation?
- What is it about this situation that is making me so uncomfortable?
- What do I fear losing in this situation?
- What am I demanding of the people around me, and why is it so upsetting that I am not getting it?
- What is the worst thing that could happen if I said or did __________?
- Why am I so worried about the possibility of people seeing me as imperfect, unhelpful, a failure, not unique, self-seeking, self-protecting, greedy, addicted, or ignorant? In some cases isn't this certainly true?
- What is the reason I am giving people the power to upset me?
- What is the most helpful thing I can do in this instance to learn about myself and the people and situation at hand?
- If I am alone, what is it that I am concentrating on in myself that is transforming solitude into loneliness and self-deprecation?
- Why am I taking an annoying event and making it into something worse?

We often don't stop to ask ourselves these basic questions that help free us from wasteful ways of thinking leading to an unhealthy perspective. We can be more content with ourselves as we travel our psychological and spiritual journeys in life. These questions are designed to break the logjam of unrealistic expectations, unnecessary fears, crippling angers, destructive anxieties, and undue distress. With practice, it becomes possible to live with greater clarity, contentment, and compassion. These questions also produce a good deal of information on how we are falling into patterns of pleasing, grasping, and controlling rather than living out of a sense of self that we are both aware of and feel congruent with.

The freedom to live with a healthier perspective has a cost: *honesty* and *humility*. Without these, we are not clear about what is before us, we fail to be content, and we often lack the purity of motivations to help us be compassionate without wanting anything in return. Yes, there is a cost, but the return is serenity. If we are aware that we have been given myriad talents (some yet unexplored), as an act of gratitude for possessing them we can seek to enhance and share them as best as we can. The process allows us to never, ever forget they are in fact originally genetic *gifts*, and so we can be excited and content to be who we are without a drop of conceit—which will also be a gift to others who encounter us.

COGNITIVE-BEHAVIORAL THEORY

As part of my theoretical preparation to put the early insight that I received from my mentor into practice, I learned about cognitive-behavioral therapy (CBT) to complement and eventually integrate with my current practice, which emphasized a more psychodynamic approach (one that was concerned more with early life influences on the present and with balancing the differing elements at play in the person's unconscious "inner life"). Cognitive-behavioral therapy provides great insights into why people feel the way they do and how both affect (your emotions) and behaviors are determined to a great extent by their cognitions (ways of thinking, perceiving, and understanding) and schemata (beliefs). Given this, CBT advises that people seeking a healthier perspective should put forth a daily effort to carefully examine their own cognitions for distortions that may be causing difficulties.

Cognitive-behavioral therapy recognizes that psychological problems are often negatively impacted by dysfunctional thinking. Originally developed by Aaron Beck in the 1960s, this short-term, structured psychotherapy was first used with clients suffering from depression but has since been expanded to include areas such as other mood disorders, trauma, substance abuse, and the improvement of everyday living. The major assumption of CBT is that life experiences create core beliefs and schemas—our underlying beliefs that provide a way of responding based on our relationship to self, others, and the world. These, in turn, drive our personal rules, attitudes, and assumptions. And so, when an incident occurs, these automatic thoughts and "rules" are generated that impact behavior and mood.

Cognitive-behavioral theory and therapy can be helpful because there is a bias for action and an emphasis on working with the present as a way to alleviate the symptoms of psychic distress as quickly as possible. As a result, we are invited by this theory to identify (by ourselves or with a wise friend/coach) a dysfunctional cognition or thought process based on some of our core beliefs and to work on decreasing negative emotions and affect while increasing coping skills related to the negative unexamined automatic thoughts: in essence, to seek a healthier perspective. The simple tenet of this theory is that we don't typically examine our thoughts or the proof we have for them: we simply accept them at face value. As a result, dysfunctional thinking can continue to operate, leading to actions and a lifestyle that could be so much richer if we had only taken the time—either on our own or with a guide—to ask ourselves the right questions when we feel negative about ourselves or a situation.

Distorted thoughts can come in a variety of forms. Examples include *catastrophizing* (I am going to lose everything); *magnifying* (this is the worst thing that could ever happen to me); *overgeneralizing* (everyone thinks this way about me); *jumping to conclusions; selective negative focus; emotional reasoning; "should," polarized, or all-or-nothing thinking* (if we don't do it my way, it is wrong); and *personalizing* (he doesn't like me because I didn't go out to lunch with him). While many people may fall into using this type of unexamined, negative thinking from time to time, it becomes especially problematic when it becomes the default way of thinking, which unfortunately may happen when we are at a low point during our lives. Yet, whether it is extreme or not, for all of us, dysfunctional thinking certainly stands in the way of possessing a healthy perspective in life.

Negative thinking is more common than we might imagine. As was illustrated earlier in the case of my patient who heard praise in a whisper, it is easier to give more weight to a negative interpretation than to anything positive. Often we hear a compliment or affirmation only to have it dissolve when negative stones are thrown and hit their mark. Thus, it is important that we learn to recognize negative thinking in order to link these thoughts to depressive or anxious feelings that may result. Then, the negative self-talk can be replaced with a more realistic thought or belief. (In addition, as we shall soon see, the use of accurate, positive language is also central to helping us make changes.)

Generally, it is easy to find something negative about ourselves and even easier to make negative comparisons with others. Maintaining a healthy perspective in light of these challenges—even though it can be an extremely worthwhile endeavor—is where the real work begins. As Rainer Maria Rilke, in one of his *Letters to a Young Poet,* observes:

> Only someone who is ready for everything, who excludes nothing, not even the most enigmatical, will live the relation to another as something alive and will himself draw exhaustively from his own existence. For if we think of this existence

> of the individual as a larger or smaller room it appears evident that most people learn to know only one corner of their room, a place by the window, a strip of floor on which they will walk up and down. Thus they have a certain security. And yet that dangerous insecurity is so much more human which drives the prisoner in Poe's stories to feel out the shapes of their horrible dungeons and not be strangers to the unspeakable terror of their abode. We, however, are not prisoners. No traps or snares are set about us, and there is nothing which should intimidate or worry us. . . . We have no reason to mistrust our world, for it is not against us. Has it terrors, they are our terrors; has it abysses, those abysses belong to us; are dangers at hand, we must try to love them.

To accomplish this form of self-awareness, so change becomes more readily possible, a number of steps can be taken, either by ourselves or with a therapist, coach, mentor, or counselor: exploring how you are interpreting an event, revisiting the emotional arousal it caused, and examining the resulting behavior that you undertook. As part of this recollection process, it is important that both the objective (what actually happened) and the subjective (what beliefs and judgments you have made about the event) be examined. With this process you can then be encouraged to uncover the style of your own thinking process as well as examine the accuracy of the conclusions you are drawing. (I will say more about this in Chapter 5.)

POSITIVE PSYCHOLOGY

With a sense of the value of CBT as a backdrop, another even more recent advance in the behavioral sciences that can be helpful—especially in gaining a healthier perspective—is *positive psychology*. Its goal is to encourage people to see the field of clinical psychology not merely as a "repair shop" for emotional difficulties (as important as this role is) but also as a resource to help people uncover their signature strengths. By drawing attention to people's gifts, talents, and virtues, people can then build on what is good instead of solely focusing on correcting what is problematic. This enhances resiliency, which is an area of importance to those wishing to have a healthier perspective.

The discipline of positive psychology is about living well. It is prevention-focused and works to expand existing competencies. It looks at people's past experiences and how they have adapted to become who they are today. It also examines their sense of personal contentment and how their attitudes and optimism influence their future. By taking this perspective, people are encouraged to question themselves in a new, more holistic way. As we saw earlier, people—and those who guide them—are sometimes stuck looking solely at their shortcomings while neglecting the power of their innate talents and gifts. Positive psychology seeks to correct this imbalance.

According to Martin Seligman, initiator of the contemporary positive psychology movement and author of *Authentic*

Happiness: Using Positive Psychology to Realize Your Potential for Lasting Fulfillment:

> The field of positive psychology at the subjective level is about positive subjective experience: well-being and satisfaction (past); flow, joy, the sensual pleasures, and happiness (present); and constructive cognitions about the future—optimism, hope, and faith. At the individual level it is about positive personal traits—the capacity for love and vocation, courage, interpersonal skill, aesthetic sensibility, perseverance, forgiveness, originality, future-mindedness, high talent, and wisdom. . . . Psychology is not just the study of disease, weakness, and damage; it also is the study of strength and virtue. Treatment is not just fixing what is wrong; it is also building what is right. . . . [T]he major strides in prevention have largely come from a perspective focused on systematically building competency, not correcting weakness. . . . This, then, is the general stance of positive psychology toward prevention. It claims that there is a set of buffers against psychopathology: the positive human traits.

Positive psychology is not a psychological concealer that hides the real blemishes of life, nor is it an emotional or spiritual cortisone that temporarily hides unpleasant life experiences. Instead, it is a more dynamic way for people to view their state of being and be freed from the bindings of a solely negative focus. Although positive psychology is centered on the individual, it also integrates the strengths of supporting institutions such as families, schools, and religious institutions.

Positive and negative emotions are designed to have specific purposes in our lives. Too much of one, without the other, could be problematic. As Christopher Peterson, the author of *A Primer on Positive Psychology*, noted,

> Negative emotions alert us to danger. When we experience a negative emotion, our response options narrow, and we act with haste to avoid whatever danger is signaled. In contrast, positive emotions signal safety, and our inherent response to them is not to narrow our options but to broaden and build upon them. The evolutionary payoff of positive emotions is therefore not in the here and now, but in the future. Perhaps it is advantageous to experience positive emotions because they lead us to engage in activities that add to our behavioral and cognitive repertoires.

Research has also shown that a positive outlook can contribute to longer, healthier lives, richer marriages, more productive work environments, and closer friendships. In addition, this optimism improves resilience, strengthens coping skills, and moves people from survival to enrichment—a movement that is clearly essential if we are to have, and live out of, a healthy perspective.

One measure of the richness of life is to consider our experience of "flow." Identified by Mihaly Csikszentmihalyi (in his book *Flow*), this psychological state of being is the overlap of refined skill, single-mindedness, and joy. For individuals who experience flow, time seems to stand still, there is no self-consciousness, and the activity brings a sense of completeness. By embarking on a discovery process that highlights our most rewarding activities and encourages a steady diet of them, we are better able to help ourselves (and others who seek our support) tap into the positive energy in and around us.

To employ positive psychology as a tool in seeking a healthier perspective, we should center our attention on experiences, events, behaviors, cognitions, gifts, talents, and conditions to be recalled, celebrated, and reinforced—not just our problems, defenses, and growing edges, as important as awareness of them might be.

Deriving honest meaning from our experiences and testing our perceptions can offer a freedom that may be unknown or elusive up to that point in our lives, because of the unexamined negative beliefs we hold. So, with both cognitive-behavioral therapy and positive psychology as a backdrop (see resources on these areas listed at the end of the book), we now turn to *reframing for change* and *signature strengths* as applied to gaining, maintaining, or regaining a healthy perspective.

REFRAMING FOR CHANGE

Cognitive reframing is an intervention that helps people create new meaning from distressing situations in which irrational, distorted, or imbalanced thinking has affected their behavior, mood, or both. With the collaboration of psychological guides or—as in the case of this book—by identifying your own maladaptive thoughts or narrow ways of viewing events, you can generate new ideas that will allow you to modify both your perception (and ultimately both feeling and behavior) and your perspective, even though the precipitating event actually remains the same. It is your view or reframing of the event that has changed.

Most dysfunctional thinking styles have taken a lifetime to develop, and people need adequate space to consider a reconceptualization of their thinking and beliefs. This cycle of cognitive appraisal, emotional arousal, and behavior is also continuous. Once again, the goal of reframing for change is not designed to deny realities but *to look into them with a sense of openness and hope—a different perspective.* It recognizes where we are in the cycle of change and brings it into clearer focus. With that awareness, we can begin connecting our maladaptive thoughts and incomplete or inaccurate personal assumptions. And by practicing reframing in- and outside of the reflective periods of "alonetime" in our day, we can derive new insights and enhance personal well-being.

The fundamental components of reframing our perspective in practice are as follows:

- Hear what we are saying and not saying to ourselves (self-talk)
- Acknowledge what we are feeling
- Help ourselves gain insight into the *full* experience

For instance, a young woman who came to see me was upset that she would impulsively blurt out how she felt with people close to her. This had cost her dearly in her interpersonal relationships. Rather than simply trying to get her to curb her tendencies, I first pointed out to her that she was a very passionate person who believed that being truthful was important. Those two elements represented signature strengths for her. The issue was that under certain circumstances those very gifts became growing edges. The goal was not to remove all of her passionate style—which would be impossible anyway—but to consider both the gift and the growing edge in terms of how and when they would be expressed.

Often we debate whether the glass is half full or half empty. In reframing, our interest is in the entire glass, both the represented signature strengths *and* our defenses/growing edges. The goal is not to hide or play down the defenses or situational challenges, but to recognize them for what they are while *simultaneously* applauding the gifts in all parts of ourselves or members of our family or those who turn to us at work for guidance.

Just as mattes and frames around a painting can bring different details to the foreground, in utilizing CBT and positive psychology, the practice of seeking a perspective that is more accurate and life giving allows us to recast certain details of our story or shed light on our faulty beliefs. And just as viewing a painting from a variety of angles brings perspective, we become an observer of the "paintings" (stories in our own lives) in order to help ourselves become more fully self-aware. This is done in order to secure or regain personal power, as well as to adopt new contexts for perceiving events in particular and our life as a whole.

The process of reframing benefits from both being open and having a good sense of humor. In addition, it is essential to have a relationship with people who are explicitly familiar with CBT and positive psychology or very balanced and healthy in their own view of life. Although there are many psychological theories and techniques that can be used to help people lead more fruitful, satisfying lives, studies have shown that it is the *relationship* between the helper and the person being guided that plays the most significant role in healing. Thus, rapport and a sense of trust are critical. And so, having a companion (either in person or through writings) who is able to help us become aware of *both* our gifts and growing edges is a special gift to us when we are seeking a healthier perspective on ourselves and our lives.

When we are psychologically stuck, it can sometimes be difficult to decipher; therefore, an open mind is also essential. From a psychological and spiritual point of view, we may be experiencing a difficulty that is often not really the "problem," so we need constant reconceptualizing through reflection or within a coaching or mentoring relationship. Embracing a "what-if" mentality can illuminate new possibilities in challenges. Likewise, employing humor appropriately can release a logjam of emotions so that self-examination doesn't become too burdensome or off-putting.

CBT and positive psychology are evidence-based theories. With practice, they can add a new dimension to the search for a healthier perspective on our own lives or in support of others on their life journey. These theories also offer a new path of exploration that may be uncharted, so gentle persistence may be necessary to deal with the forward and backward steps during the entire process of seeking greater openness and flexibility to change. And finally, we must not forget that in the end, no matter how efficacious our approach, it is in the end about *experiencing* the gifts of life wherever and whenever they appear. We are imperfect, and our best intentions may fall short. Life tends to bridge those gaps and enriches the shared journey by encouraging us all to be open to "make all things new," including, maybe *especially*, ourselves.

SIGNATURE STRENGTHS

Another way to gain self-insight and a new perspective on ourselves is by identifying and cultivating our signature strengths (see Box 5). Timothy Hodges, executive director of the Gallup University, and Donald Clifton, author of a number of quite helpful books on strength-based living, help in this regard by providing the following definition of a strength: "the ability to provide consistent, near-perfect performance in a given activity. The key to building a strength is to first identify your dominant themes of talent, then to discover your specific talents within

Box 5 Aspects of Positive Psychology and Emotions That Aid in Gaining a Healthier, More Balanced Perspective on Oneself

- As Barbara Frederickson, author of the book *Positivity* and one of the leading researchers on the topic of human flourishing, notes, each person's pathway to living fully is unique, so becoming aware of our own personality strengths and personal joyful pursuits is an essential and worthwhile undertaking.
- Positive emotions encourage the development of a more creative and healthier perspective as well as lead to new, effective actions. Unlike negative emotions, such as fear or anger, which prepare us for specific actions (run or attack), positive emotions, such as optimism, happiness, and gratitude open us up to a broader cognitive and behavioral repertoire. In essence, the message is this: if you attend to only negative emotions, you will survive. But if you *also* attend to positive ones, you will not only raise the chances of your survival, but you will also have greater problem-solving abilities and truly "live," rather than merely "exist."
- Positive psychology helps us look beyond our dark side. In an effort to be more fully self-aware, it is advantageous if we recognize, as leading positive psychologist, Christopher Peterson, suggests, that "what is good in life is as genuine as what is bad and not simply the absence of what is problematic."

- As Distinguished Scientist Award winner Ed Diener recognizes, problem solving does not simply take on the negative; it also builds on the positive.
- An interest in flourishing has us focus on self-appreciation and acceptance; an interest in our own development; a desire to find and follow a mission in life that will benefit not only us but others; a recognition of the value of mastering certain elements in our life; an honoring of one's own personal ethic; and an understanding of what factors (for example, empathy) would expand and deepen our personal relationships (Ryff, 1989).
- Positive emotions can lead to new creative solutions, whereas negative emotions, because they are so narrowly focused, are not able to jump-start broader problem-solving and innovative actions.
- Because psychology is not simply a study of how to fix what is broken, we must attend not only to our growing edges and defenses but also to our strengths, talents, and virtues. We do this not only because it will help to balance the picture, but also because our very gifts can be very positive tools in facing difficult issues.
- When we experience positive emotions as the result of novel approaches (creativity, resilience, optimism, humor, etc.) in the short term, these experiences are held in store for the long term as well. So, reinforcements have lasting power in the long run and provide a positive memory of success (mastery, autonomy, positive relations with others, and psychological agility).

those themes, and lastly to refine them with knowledge and skills."

Some strengths and talents may be readily apparent, such as the student who can organize and lead a group of individuals to accomplish a task regardless of whether it is a science lab or a campus-wide rally. Another may be able to electrify an audience, because of his ability to speak clearly and passionately about his area of interest or expertise. For still others, personality clues may have to be sorted to determine predominant strengths. Cambridge-educated Marcus Buckingham and Donald Clifton, for example, in their work speak about spontaneous reactions, yearnings, rapid learning, and satisfaction as possible ways of identifying talent. In other words, what are your gut reactions, what are you drawn to doing, how quickly do you pick up a new skill, and what makes you happy?

A resource designed by Christopher Peterson and Marty Seligman, called the Character Strengths and Virtues Classification System, is worth consulting because it offers a means of thinking about what is inherently good in people, which happens to contribute to their resilience, meaning, and happiness. Briefly, the system isolates key characteristics of a strength, including the following: consistently evident and stable over time; valued by society; nurtured by caregivers; promoted through structured institutions such as schools; identified by role models, as well as prodigies; and recognized and highly regarded by most major cultures.

In Peterson and Seligman's guide, six virtues are identified and divided into twenty-four subcategories representing character strengths:

1. *Wisdom and knowledge* combined represent the mental fitness to solicit and utilize information. Suggested strengths include curiosity, interest; love of learning; judgment, critical thinking, open-mindedness; practical intelligence, creativity, originality, ingenuity, and perspective.
2. *Courage* is the emotional tenacity that drives achievement regardless of the obstacles. Strengths highlighted are in the areas of valor; industry, perseverance; integrity, honesty, authenticity, and zest and enthusiasm.
3. *Love* is self-sacrifice for another. Strengths involve intimacy, reciprocal attachment; kindness, generosity, nurturance; social intelligence, personal intelligence, and emotional intelligence.
4. *Justice* refers to the desire to complete civic duties that contribute to the larger whole. This includes citizenship, duty, loyalty, teamwork; equity, fairness, and leadership.
5. *Temperance* refrains from excess and includes strengths such as forgiveness, mercy, modesty, humility, prudence, caution, self-control, and self-regulation.
6. *Transcendence* ties to that which is greater than the self and gives humankind purpose. Strengths include awe, wonder, appreciation of beauty and excellence; gratitude; hope, optimism, future-mindedness; playfulness, humor; spirituality, sense of purpose, faith, and religiousness.

This list provides a framework in which to explore these in ourselves. Christopher Peterson and Marty Seligman suggest the following activities to cultivate virtues and strengths:

- Brainstorming ideas for an express purpose promotes creativity.
- Taking risks, adapting, and questioning are ways of building courage.
- Incorporating fun encourages perseverance.
- Participating in community service promotes social responsibility.
- Practicing forgiveness of self and others rather than holding on to the hurt and blame releases new energy.
- Offering accurate feedback encourages humility and modesty, if it is stated in a manner that allows the individual to grow.
- Laughing brings about playfulness.
- Thanking others for no reason at all grows gratitude.

Many of these activities can be expanded to include a larger community, whether it is our extended family, the workplace, or an institution (church, school, etc.) in which we are involved.

Another way to look at strengths in depth is to complete "A Questionnaire for Self-Reflection on Personal Strengths and Virtues" (see Box 6; these questions will replace the end of chapter section "Some Questions to Consider at This Point…"). Originally found in my book *Bounce,* on maximizing one's resiliency range, given its potentially significant impact on

Box 6 A Questionnaire for Self-Reflection on Personal Strengths and Virtues

Introduction

There are a number of Web sites that have online surveys on positive psychology (for example, www.authentichappiness.org is connected with Martin Seligman's book *Authentic Happiness*). Many books include exercises as a result of research in this field. Chief among these books are Peterson's *A Primer in Positive Psychology*, Seligman's *Authentic Happiness,* and Boldt's *Pursuing Human Strengths.* Others are also listed at the end of this book. They have been developed by the current leaders in the field and can strengthen your ability to embrace life more fully.

The questions that follow have been formulated to inspire reflection on the way we perceive and live our lives. A secondary goal is to increase your interest in reading further with an eye to deepening your own capacity and sense of fulfillment.

The overarching aim of these goals is to enhance the paradigm for self-evaluation so that the way you look at yourself is not simply based on the negative: preventing, limiting, or ameliorating negative or unproductive ways of perceiving life, or eliminating unhelpful habits, traits, or interpersonal styles. Instead, I hope the process of filling out this questionnaire will allow you to view yourself in a more balanced, potent, and accurate light. The result of this? A more healthy

(*continued*)

Box 6 (Continued)

pursuit of human strengths and virtues that, in turn, could lead to a more profound appreciation of a fuller life for you; your family, friends, and coworkers; and those you serve or who count on you. The interpersonal circle you share with others can then be gracefully completed by your broader, positive sense of self because, once again, one of the greatest gifts you can share with others is a sense of your own peace, joy, and hope, and a healthy perspective, which grows from an understanding of your strengths and virtues. But you cannot share fully if you are not fully aware of these talents. You cannot be *the calm within the storm*. It is as simple as that.

Questions for Consideration

Which persons and situations make life more joyful and meaningful for you?

How do you enhance and nurture these relationships and situations?

What do you consider to be your most important personal and occupational/professional goals? Are they yours, or have you "inherited" them from others in your family or circle of friends?

How are you enjoying/flowing with the process of your efforts to achieve this?

What are your major strengths and virtues? (Asking family, friends, and coworkers might help you to obtain a broader and more in-depth list.)

How do you seek to apply these virtues and signature strengths in daily life?
What are your particular personal and professional/occupational talents?
How do you foster their use—especially in enhancing your ongoing relationships with others?
What do you feel are the positive motivations for you to become and remain committed personally and occupationally?
What are your strategies for facing obstacles to your professional and personal growth?
In what way do your own challenges or the suffering of other people enable you to deepen and appreciate your life more fully—no matter what difficulties you may be facing?
What are some new experiences that you were open to recently that you felt were broadening to you, either at home or at work?
What are some recent illustrations of how you were able to recognize your own emotions and creatively employ them in an interpersonal situation?
What are some of the approaches you use to remove obstacles to your own growth?
In terms of your own strengths and virtues, what are illustrations of you at your best as a person?
How are these strengths and virtues connected with your overall philosophy as to what would make your life worth living?

(*continued*)

Box 6 (Continued)

How are you reinforcing these strengths and virtues?

What is the connection for you between exercising these strengths and

- the development of rewarding relationships,
- your sense of well-being as a person, and
- your sense of "psychological efficacy" (the power and control you feel in life)?

How has your own resiliency on the job and at home actually been enhanced rather than diminished by very challenging encounters?

In looking over your own life, what has made you value your own life more deeply?

What ideas and beliefs do you believe enables you and others to flourish as human beings?

What are some of the ways in which you ensure your autonomy personally and occupationally/professionally?

Given your personal mission/career goals in life, what is your specific plan to achieve them?

In what ways do you ensure balance in your professional and personal life?

How would you describe your style of relating to those with whom you are most deeply connected?

What is it that others find most endearing about you?

Which of the following traits do you possess and value? (Place a check mark next to each one below that relates to you; after doing so, go back and give a double check mark for those that especially stand out for you.)

Dependable
Responsible
Open
Flexible
Welcoming
Trustworthy
Friendly
Hopeful
Understanding
Warm
Mature
Enjoyable to be with
Sympathetic
Encouraging
Energetic
A problem-solver
A conflict-resolver
Forgiving
Able to postpone gratification
Self-aware
Able to consider the greater good
Happy
Enthusiastic
Willing to listen

(*continued*)

Box 6 (Continued)

- Strong
- Lifelong learner
- Considerate
- Romantic
- Committed
- Confident
- Emotionally stable
- Industrious
- Sociable
- Empathic
- Able to form close relationships
- Able to set aside time for reflection, silence, and solitude
- Can easily share thoughts, feelings, and hopes with others
- Can monitor and regulate my own strong emotions
- Deals well with ambiguities and surprises
- Able to set priorities and follow them
- Sees happiness, as opposed to pleasures, as important and knows what contributes to it
- Sees mindfulness practices as valuable in my life
- Has a balanced circle of friends
- Able to laugh at myself
- Optimistic

What are some interesting ways you can use the above talents/gifts/strengths in unique ways in your personal life and at work?

What institutions (e.g., universities, healthcare facilities, religious/community/political organizations, professional associations) are you involved in, and what are the benefits both to you and the institutions themselves from your efforts?

If an article were written about you at the end of your life, what would you want included in it?

As you reflect on your life, for whom and what are you most grateful in your personal and professional/occupational life? (Please be detailed.)

What are ways that you savor good experiences in your personal and professional/occupational life? (Provide illustrations.)

What are your favorite leisure activities, and how do you fit them in your schedule?

How do you increase the frequency of your contact with enjoyable/stimulating/encouraging/inspiring/humorous friends?

Given positive psychology's philosophy of viewing your gifts and talents as clearly as your growing edges, what other questions would you need/like to ask yourself to open up a greater appreciation of the positive aspects of your personal life and enhance the meaningfulness of the work you do?

Source: R. Wicks, *Bounce: Living the Resilient Life* (New York: Oxford University Press, 2008).

the gaining or regaining of a healthy perspective, it is included again here.

The questions in it are designed to inspire self-exploration and whet the appetite to delve further into the subject. The mere practice of identifying strengths and offering examples of how they have been used can be extremely gratifying especially during tough times. It is also good to be reminded of all the gifts that we have because some that may have fallen out of practice can still be of great value to us.

The ability for people to be proficient at something—or perhaps even be an expert—can contribute to happiness and well-being. Thus, uncovering our strengths, as well as finding ways in which we can employ our talents in daily life, is essential for instilling confidence and supporting mastery. Dieter Frey developed his own principles of leadership and motivation highlighting central themes that positively influenced employee satisfaction and performance in the workplace. These principles are an outgrowth of human strengths and offer a framework for another way of intervening in not only our own lives but in others' as well. Likewise, the questions that follow each principle can offer a means to ongoing introspection:

- *Providing meaning and vision.* People who perceive their work as having a greater purpose and tied to a larger strategy are more motivated and enthusiastic about what they do. (How do I see my role as a helper to others? How do my particular strengths benefit my family, friends, school, religious organization, or workplace? How clearly am I able to link my actions to the broader strategy of organizations of which I am a part?)

- *Transparency*. Being informed helps people have a sense of control and provides a framework for change. (Are the discussions with others in the family, community, or workplace open and honest? Can constructive criticism be shared and valued? Is this echoed in my organization?)
- *Participation and autonomy*. People who actively contribute to the decision-making process are more likely to assume responsibility. (What are the expectations of any mentoring-type relationship of which I am a part? Am I invested and willing to work diligently together with those who guide me or with those I am called to guide?)
- *Sense of fit*. If people understand their strengths and use them to do the work they love, they will be more motivated to keep doing it. (Do I have the skills necessary and the interest? What are my motivations? Are they a good fit for the type of work I do and family life I have?)
- *Goal setting and goal negotiation*. People who establish reasonable goals and develop a plan to meet them tend to be more motivated. (Are there specific goals established for my personal development? Is there enough flexibility to re-evaluate the goals as necessary and resources to accomplish what I have laid out?)
- *Constructive feedback and appreciation*. People want to do well and be recognized. Likewise, positive correction builds people

and their skills. (Is there room for my ongoing appraisal individually? Is this support echoed in my place of work, where I volunteer, etc.?)

- *Professional and social integration.* People want to be part of a community and acknowledged for their contributions. (How is this need fulfilled in my life at this point? How do I model having a healthy perspective in my life?)
- *Personal growth.* People want to expand their skills and knowledge. (How am I encouraging personal growth in myself?)
- *Situational leadership.* Leadership style is adaptable to the event and should be clear and directive. (How am I seeking to enhance my own strengths as a leader in my family? With various community organizations? At work?)
- *Fair and equitable material reward.* This suggests that rewards should be clearly articulated and commensurate with the investment. (What are the tangible and intangible rewards of having a more positively balanced view of myself and the world?)

These exploratory questions are a suggested guide for personal reflection about growth, mastery, and contentment. This rich body of information can be leveraged throughout our own personal development process and beyond. Several applications suggest themselves (each will be discussed in the following pages):

- Doing a holistic self-assessment that includes your gifts as well as your growing edges
- Making a choice with an appreciation that we just don't think our way into a new kind of thinking but must also act

our way into a new kind of living (as the Twelve Steps of AA would suggest)

- Practicing new behavior that will encourage growth and openness, such as seeking to find a positive aspect of yourself or others each time only a negative, narrow assessment comes to mind
- Paying it forward by behaving toward others as we now are behaving toward ourselves
- Partnering with others who are models of maintaining or regaining a healthy perspective after it is temporarily lost
- Viewing each day as our last, since such an appreciation of our own impermanence encourages us not to get caught in petty struggles

Although there are benefits to doing these activities individually, they can become an even richer experience when done collectively because they foster new discoveries and ongoing refinement.

Conducting an honest self-assessment is also a foundational step to using positive psychology in an effort to gain a healthier perspective on self and the world. A fair appraisal of strengths, growing edges, and attitude is necessary to make minute and incremental improvements. Given this, how do we respond to questions such as these:

- Do we characterize life as full of opportunity or a problem to endure?

- If we generally have a positive mindset, then what tips the scale toward a negative mindset? Do some situations or individuals especially sap our energy?
- If we become exhausted, how can our interactions be limited or changed going forward to create better outcomes?
- If a negative mindset is more the norm for us at a given point, do we remember that cognitive restructuring and reframing takes time, care, and patience but is well worth the effort?

Choice is another key driver in using positive psychology and the development of a healthier perspective. In other words, we need to intentionally choose to employ strengths in life and use the lens of positivity to view all that happens. Often people are trapped in a thought process that says, "I have to do it this way," or "If I can just survive this, I can get to the next better thing." This thought process influences our behavior consciously and unconsciously. We may procrastinate, worry about something that is out of our control, or be wrought with anxiety that far outweighs the actual situation. In essence, we are robbing ourselves of joy when we do not recognize that we can govern our behavior.

Take a moment to consider all of the things that are "obligations" on the calendar. How can they become opportunities to learn something new, as well as to help nourish the growth of another individual? Also, consider what is done well and *liked*. Many people can be trained to do things so well that they can be perceived as strengths. However, they may not enjoy spending hours in those activities. This is often true in the workplace, where people must adapt to retain their employment. Thus, determine how more time can be spent doing activities that utilize signature strengths. For example, being a mentor to colleagues energizes some, while for others ensuring they are at their children's sport/club event gives them meaning.

Practicing is still another key concept. Cultivating strengths by employing them often and using them in unique ways is critical. In addition, it is helpful to consider how a positive attitude impacts the way a strength is used or how a negative attitude may minimize what is inherently good. It is easy for us to start complaining when everyone else in the room is doing so and to be swept away by hopelessness in difficult, tragic, or chronic situations. Yet, those individuals who can draw something of value from any situation have a tendency to do better and remain healthier than those who cannot. And so, it is not Pollyannaish (as some may claim) to practice by looking for the good in yourself, others, and events. For example, weather often brings about a lot of comments, usually negative—but it doesn't have to be this way. For instance, you can simply respond in ways that illustrate how you use a rainy day productively or how a change in seasons is something you enjoy.

Whenever possible, include others by *paying it forward* as a wonderfully beneficial way to put positive psychology to use in your own life as well as in the lives of others. Strengths used to benefit a community have a tendency to grow because they are called on more frequently and praised. Likewise, individuals who can highlight the strengths of others are in a position to give gifts of immeasurable worth. People in our lives who come to us with great hurts may not be receiving very many nurturing deposits from those in their interpersonal network. Whenever we can help them recognize their courage for walking through our door, their tenacity for continuing their visits, and their strength in working through their challenges, we are instrumental in beginning the healing process for them—and this is a powerful way to develop the signature strengths in ourselves!

Most of us have unique opportunities throughout the day to put in a word that can go a long way in providing encouragement, but because of our perspective on the "helping process," we may miss out on those small but possibly significant moments. Small, daily steps can matter in surprising ways when we go beyond simply thinking about good acts and actually do them. For example, complimenting at least one person a day about something that makes them special can have an unexpected positive impact.

One way of doing this is looking at the details. Does a friend wear a hat celebrating his service to our country or an organization pin on her lapel? Both suggest a willingness to sacrifice and serve others, which are incredible gifts. Another way is catching them in the act of doing something positive or beneficial. For example, a gentle and generous colleague of mine was out to dinner with her family and saw a young father with three boys ranging in age from about five to ten. It was a busy evening, and they waited a long time for their food. As she and her family left, she told the father and his sons how impressed she was with their kind and caring behavior to each other. Dad sat up a bit straighter and thanked her. Each of the boys beamed. That was a fleeting interaction, but for those few moments she and they enjoyed what was strong and good in their family—and in her, since she manifested one of her own signature strengths: demonstrating compassion for others.

There are many people around who would be pleased to share what they know and *partner with us.* The easiest way to improve on a particular strength is by joining another who desires the same. This can occur in two ways: choosing a partner whose skill is a few levels higher, to foster growth, not frustration; or finding someone who could model and teach us. If positivity is a struggle, we need to spend time with people who have a healthier perspective than we do. Consider how they act, speak, and carry themselves. Observe how they make others feel when we are with them. Then we must take the further effort to adapt/imitate what they do. We may find this awkward at first, but it will become more natural over time.

Finally, *view each day as the last.* Our lives on this earth are finite, yet we often act as if they are eternal. We allow anger to fester, deny forgiveness, and foster dysfunction. We toss away precious moments surfing the net or watching television instead of investing in relationships. Would we still do that if we knew that this was our last day on earth? Chances are a few things would change and we would focus on making good memories and getting closure. And so, we need to make a commitment to stop and be mindful throughout the day; choose to operate from a source of strength; and, finally, select words and act in ways that build others up, not pull them down.

By integrating aspects of positive psychology, including contentment, growth, and mastery in our own lives as well as in significant relationships, gifts of untold value may be unwrapped through gaining a balanced picture (*both* gifts and growing edges) of those who come to us for guidance as well as ourselves. Seeking to have a more balanced, fuller view of self can be also an opportunity to identify and sharpen strengths and sets the stage to expand the story we have of ourselves, our "narrative." Thus, we now turn to a few lessons from the narrative therapy literature that can help us gain a healthier perspective on ourselves and, in turn, those we encounter.

NARRATIVE THERAPY

At each phase of our lives—not just once and for all—we need to maintain a healthy perspective on life that includes the way we view *ourselves*, rather than simply mimicking what others say about us. In Parker Palmer's book *Let Your Life Speak*, he reflects on the favorable elements of his own life: "The life I am living is not the same as the life that wants to live in me.... I had started to understand that it is indeed possible to live a life other than one's own.... I had simply found a 'noble' way to live that was not my own, a life spent imitating heroes instead of listening to my heart." On a more dramatic note, actress Liv Ullman once shared the following deeply felt sentiment regarding her own narrative: "I am learning that if I just go on accepting the framework for life that others have given me, if I fail to make my own choices, the reasons for my life will be missing. I will be unable to recognize that which I have the power to change. I refuse to spend my life regretting the things I failed to do."

What Palmer and Ullman are both struggling with is the narrative of their lives. A very creative approach to achieving a healthier, richer sense of self is with *narrative therapy*. Narrative therapy as a process is associated with the groundbreaking work of Michael White and David Epston. They were interested in how people's life stories attributed *to* them, but not *by* them, were problematic. In one of their key maxims, "The person is not the problem, the problem is the problem." And the problem is a function of a labeling that overshadows alternative stories of possibility that people have within themselves but may not be in touch with at the time.

This is not simply the case in clinical settings but in how we perceive life, *our* lives, in all settings. Once again, in the words of educator and author Parker Palmer,

> When we lose track of true self, how can we pick up the trail? One way is to seek clues in stories from our younger years, years when we lived closer to our birthright gifts. A few years ago, I found some clues to myself in a time machine of sorts.

A friend sent me a tattered copy of my high school newspaper.... [I said in it] that I would become a naval aviator and then take up a career in advertising.

I was indeed "wearing other people's faces," and I can tell you exactly whose they were. My father worked with a man who had once been a navy pilot. He was Irish, charismatic, romantic, full of the wild blue yonder and a fair share of the blarney and I wanted to be like him. The father of one of my boyhood friends was in advertising, and though I did not yearn to take on his persona, which was too buttoned-down for my taste, I did yearn for the fast car and other large toys that seemed to be the accessories of his selfhood!

These self-prophecies now over forty years old, seem wildly misguided for a person who eventually became a Quaker, a would-be pacifist, a writer, and an activist. Taken literally, they illustrate how early in life we can lose track of who we are. But inspected through the lens of paradox, my desire to become an aviator and an advertiser contain clues to the core of true self that would take many years to emerge: clues, by definition, are coded and must be deciphered.... From the beginning, our lives lay down clues to selfhood and vocation, though the clues may be hard to decode. But trying to interpret them is profoundly worthwhile—especially when we are in our twenties or thirties or forties, feeling profoundly lost, having wandered, or been dragged, far away from our birthright gifts.

Narrative therapy encourages the very skills that all of us need to have in opening up our perspective as to who we are, who we can be, and how we might live each day. And this includes our vocation and long-term goals. Some skills worth practicing with these goals in mind are

- listening to our hopes, dreams, and ideas so they are not eclipsed or crushed by the attitudes of culture, family, work, or our own previously limited self-definition;
- reflecting on those "little" events and experiences that gave and give us joy so they can be given further opportunities for expression;
- having a chance to reframe our difficulties in light of possibly unexplored gifts and talents;
- giving ourselves the power to author our own stories, since we—not others—hold the "copyright" to our identity;
- being sensitive to our self-talk (what we mentally tell ourselves about events, people, and ourselves) in order to pick up interpretations and criticism that are centered not in us but in the outside world's set of values and ethics;
- opening ourselves to an array of stories that color our lives (volunteer work may not be considered "important" because the culture doesn't seem to value unpaid activities, but after exploration *we* may see the good we are doing and the joy it may be bringing us) but have been underrated; and
- participating in rituals/activities that reinforce and stabilize new, more life-giving identities.

Narrative therapeutic views help us to see more and more of life anew in ways that help our perspective to become more open to possibility. This is done by isolating assumptions we have about ourselves, examining them, and considering alternative views—especially ones developed by *us* and not merely a mimicking of other authority figures (parents, educators, the predominant culture, therapists, etc.) no matter how noble their intentions may be.

As Stephen Madigan, author of a small work on the approach (*Narrative Therapy*), notes,

> From the beginning, a central poststructural tenet of narrative therapy was the idea that we as persons are "multi-storied."...Simply stated, narrative therapists took up the position that within the context of therapy, there could be numerous interpretations about persons and problems....And the very interpretations of persons and problems that therapists bring forward are mediated through prevailing ideas held by our culture regarding the specifics of who and what these persons and problems are and what they represent (abnormal/normal, good/bad, worthy/unworthy).

Madigan recognized that people have a reputation with themselves that is very much in line with prevailing ideologies and, in the extreme, prejudices or opinions that have nothing to do with their own values. The goal of narrative therapy is to look at many stories/interpretations in people's lives so they can resist being cast in a way that has possibly held them back. This is exactly what we should wish for ourselves and put into practice by embracing a healthy perspective on life and an openness to new views and necessary change (see Box 7).

Furthermore, the surprises that exploring our own narrative can provide not only open us up to expanding our own self views and horizons, but they also set the stage for undertaking a fuller appreciation of the essential role for gratefulness and happiness in how we live. It is to this topic—in our efforts to enhance a healthier perspective on life—that we turn next.

Box 7 Key Practices on Expanding Our Own Narrative and Redefining Our Story

- *Re-authoring our conversations* involves identifying and attending to those parts of your life that are not in the forefront, may be neglected, or have been discouraged by others and maybe eventually by you. PRACTICE: Bring into the forefront stories of successes, joys, interesting activities, and actions worth being proud of that are now in the shadows of your awareness.
- *Bring into greater awareness new balanced storylines* other than the ones you or others usually tell about you. PRACTICE: Use a psychological approach similar to the one used in dermatology: "If it is wet, dry it; if it is dry, wet it." In other words, if people see you as an introvert, reflect on those

(*continued*)

Box 7 (Continued)

times and places in which you have been outgoing; if you are characterized or think of yourself as an extrovert, reflect and highlight those times during the day, week, and life in which you are more contemplative, quiet, and reflective.

- *Develop a list of favorable conditions* for the underenjoyed parts of yourself to develop further. PRACTICE: Assemble a prospectus of those actions—start with small steps first—that if enacted would enrich your life and enhance your storyline. For each action, also list the factors that would encourage success.
- *Reflect on persons in your life* who saw you differently and/or in a more positive light and therefore interacted with you in ways that brought out other interpersonal elements in you that are present but often are underexpressed. PRACTICE: Imagine these people in your life now inviting you to practice new, and heretofore not fully expressed, behaviors and attitudes.
- *Risk seeing yourself in different ways* other than how you/others now/did view you. PRACTICE: Picture yourself describing the adventure of seeing yourself and practicing different behaviors not normally attributed to you. For instance, if you are seen by others as a workaholic, practice taking time during the day to enjoy a leisurely walk and imagine

having encouraging people from your past rejoicing with you in your living a more balanced life.

- *Seek to appreciate more and more that recognizing and responding to negative messages* you have received about yourself (maybe even from yourself) is an essential part of balancing your own story and making the perspective you have on your life more accurate. PRACTICE: Write down people's attempts—even those who seemingly meant well—to instill fear, shame, guilt, hopelessness, a discouragement of initiative, helplessness, and unreasonable and unhelpful perfectionism (as opposed to being inspired to reach higher goals). After this, write down stories reflecting experiences of courage, stamina, self-improvement, self-understanding, forgiveness, and initiative, and recall those in your life who reinforced positive narratives.

Note: For broader and more in-depth treatment of practices in expanding your narratives, see White's *Re-authoring Lives: Interviews and Essays*; *Narrative Therapy in Practice*, edited by Monk, Winslade, Crocket, and Epston; Freedman and Combs's *Narrative Therapy*; and Madigan's *Narrative Therapy*.

THREE

Preventing "Spiritual Alzheimer's"

Understanding the Modern Psychology of Gratitude and Happiness

Grateful thinking fosters the savoring of positive life experiences and situations, so that people can extract the maximum possible satisfaction and enjoyment from their circumstances. Counting one's blessings may directly counteract the effects of... taking the good things in their lives for granted.

Robert A. Emmons, *Thanks!*

By happiness *I mean here a deep sense of flourishing that arises from an exceptionally healthy mind... a way of interpreting the world, since while it may be difficult to change the world, it is always possible to change the way we look at it.*

Matthieu Ricard, *Happiness*

Alzheimer's disease is devastating to observe or experience. You can see the sadness in the family of its victims and, in the early stages, people suffering from it also have some awareness of what is going on within them. The word that comes to mind when we think of Alzheimer's is *tragic.*

Yet when we encounter family and caregivers of persons suffering from this disease, as I have in my own work on the prevention of *secondary stress* (the pressures experienced in reaching out to help others), we can also see the beautiful commitment, strength, and hope in the eyes and actions of these wonderful caregivers. It is inspirational to see how they respect the dignity of the person experiencing Alzheimer's disease. If only we would be like them in the case of the much less dramatic but very debilitating interior counterpart with respect to one's perspective on life—"*spiritual Alzheimer's*": the incremental loss of the ability to be grateful and joyful about the daily gifts of life—no matter what the circumstances of our lives at that moment.

The famous Vietnamese Zen monk Thich Nhat Hahn once shared this insight in an interview in *Common Boundary* magazine in 1989, "During the Vietnam War we were so busy helping the wounded that we sometimes forgot to smell the flowers. Night has a very pleasant smell in Vietnam, especially in the country. But we would forget to pay attention to the smell of mint, coriander, thyme, and sage." This statement calls us to appreciate that, with the right perspective, we can see the many gifts before us that are so easy to miss. As pianist Artur Rubinstein once commented, "Happiness can only be felt if you don't set any conditions." A healthy perspective, gratitude, and happiness form a circle of grace, each enhancing the other.

Sometimes we find this grace reflected in literature. Early on in the novel *The Paris Wife*, Ernest Hemingway's wife is sitting near the water observing fishermen who were stringing fish (*goujon*) and immediately flash frying them on the spot. She says, "I bought a handful wrapped in newspaper and sat on the wall watching the barges move under Pont Sully. The nest of fish was crisp under a coarse snow of salt and smelled so simple and good. I thought it might save my life. Just a little. Just for the moment." If only we all could see our daily events in this life-giving way.

Robert A. Emmons, probably one of the most eminent researchers on gratitude today, puts it this way in his very accessible and compelling book *Thanks!*: "The human mind contains mental tools that appear to work against the tendency to perceive grace. We are forgetful. We take things for granted. We have high expectations. We assume that we are totally responsible for all the good that comes our way. After all, we have earned it. We deserve it."

Brother David Steindl-Rast, who lived through the blitzkrieg of World War II, in his book *Gratefulness,* offers a similar sentiment. He notes that most people leave the house each day with a list, and on that list is predetermined exactly what they will be grateful for. His advice is to throw away the list in order to be open to all that is there for us *if* we have the "eyes of surprise" (or what I would call *perspective*) to see. In his words, "Even the predictable turns into surprise the moment we stop taking it for granted.... Surprise is no more than a beginning of that fullness we call gratefulness. Do we find it difficult to imagine that gratefulness could ever become our basic attitude toward life? In moments of surprise we catch at least a glimpse of the joy to which gratefulness opens the door. More than that—in moments of surprise we already have a foot in the door."

Daily mindful gratitude also allows us to fully enjoy, and be renewed by, the so-called little things in life. Sensitivity to such gifts as these is an important part of having a healthy perspective on life and our ultimate sense of happiness, and recent psychological studies on gratefulness bear this out (see "Reading a Bit Further" at the end of the book.) This was also instilled in me a long time ago by fortunate circumstances in my own life.

GRATITUDE: THE SECOND RISK

As a youngster raised in the city, I learned about the need to be all that I could be in life. I was told to expand my horizons, to be willing to risk failure by reaching higher and higher. Rejection had to be faced head-on. Accepting what was "a sure bet" was not good enough.

Given my personality, I responded to this challenge, even though I felt failure keenly. I remember trying my hand at writing a weekly column in high school (all copies of which I now hope have been burned!). Other steps in this process of risking included becoming a Marine Corps officer, marrying someone I felt was much more spiritually mature than I was, applying to a doctoral program that I knew would accept only 7 out of 360 applicants, writing books for respected publishers, going into Cambodia to help the Khmer people rebuild their country after years of terror and torture, and working with physicians, nurses, and psychologists treating returning, critically injured military personnel at Walter Reed Army Hospital. As I look back, I see that I did accept the challenge to be as much of who I could be. I did deal with failure upon failure on this road, even though I felt it deeply since I am so thin-skinned. However, I now realize that going in over my head and not settling for less is not—as I thought it was in the past—the most important and challenging risk I would need to take to live fully.

The road now involves taking a much more subtle, and somehow more demanding, risk. The question that haunts me now is no longer, What *more* do I need to do to be satisfied with my life? Instead, I face the second, more profound, countercultural risk: to appreciate who and what is *already* there in my life. The greater, more crucial calling for me now is to be content with who and where I already am. Not to do so would be to miss so much with which I have been graced.

Whereas I learned to appreciate the first risk in the intense, competitive environment of New York City, the seeds of how to approach the second risk were initially planted in the country. Each summer I experienced a different pace of life and a style of living in a rural setting that many of us in the city might consider basic and unworthy of any real gratitude or excitement. We valued eating a hot breakfast, doing the hard work of baling hay and moving it into the barn, running to see a cow giving birth to her calf, falling asleep while sitting under a tree watching the sun set, or enjoying a glass of homemade cider on a Friday evening with family and friends from another farm. These were but a few of the available gifts that quite possibly would be "no big deal" to others.

I also felt this difference on one of my later trips to lecture in Newfoundland as I drove around the little picturesque town of Corner Brook in the western part of this most eastern province of Canada. As I drove along the ocean and took in the tough landscape that survived the sometimes brutal winters, I felt peace. I had a sense of knowing that the movements of the seasons didn't just mean a change in clothes but that life was something beautiful, if only I had the eyes to appreciate the gifts of each season. I needed to learn again and again the value of looking out the window in the morning and seeing what is—not moaning about what it could or should be.

During my summers on the farm in Liberty, New York, I explored our seventy-eight acres of forest and open fields and went down to the stream to look for crayfish. I caught a glimpse of a woodchuck popping its head out of its hole and then waddling off to find food. Deer moved by me in the early mornings; crows would caw overhead. It was good spending part of my growing up time this way, and I think it helped me take in the simple rural spirit, to learn elements of a "country psychology" that in later years I would see described in various, yet somehow similar, ways by spiritual writers and in books on the psychology of gratefulness and mindfulness. I had been given it all here. I had been presented with the lens of simplicity and contentment early in life; now I just had to know when to periodically pick it up again—especially when I was in danger of losing my appreciation of all the "little things" I received that I might be tempted to dismiss because of my desire for the ever expanding "more" that our consumer society convinces us we need to be happy.

RECOGNIZING THE DANGERS OF "GRATEFULNESS TOLERANCE": SEEKING A NEW PERSPECTIVE OF APPRECIATION

While I was spending summers in the country, my dad would try to come up on the weekends. Since he drove a truck all week and hated the idea of driving on his time off, he didn't own a car. He would catch a ride with my uncle Jack, and they would usually arrive after I was already asleep.

On one of these weekends, though, my father came to my room and woke me up. I still remember the nightlight and him sitting at the edge of the bed smiling. He had in his hand what looked to be an off-white case about twenty inches long. It was made of hard plastic, but at the time I thought it was made of ivory. He handed it to me and motioned for me to open it. Inside was a beautiful, dark-red, felt container and in it a beautiful musket. It was only a popgun, which shot a cork that was attached by a string, but it remains in my memory as one of the most precious gifts I have ever received.

Surprisingly, when I was in my twenties and living with an older couple on a farm just a few miles from my boyhood farm, I would have a similar experience. I was suffering from a terrible cold and decided to take a nap. After a couple of hours in bed, I heard an almost inaudible knock at the door. When I said, "Come in," the woman who owned the house stuck her head in and said, "Are you up to having a hot cup of tea and a slice of homemade blueberry pie?" When I nodded yes, she closed the door, and I got dressed and went down to the kitchen. I remember sitting at that table, the tea warming me inside, and eating what I still think is the richest piece of blueberry pie I have ever had. Just like the surprise in childhood, this small gift gave me such a large experience of life that it makes me ask to this day, "What happened to such simple, powerful moments when we were able to enjoy life to the fullest?"

Psychiatrist Gerald May, in his book *The Dark Night of the Soul* (one of the final books he wrote before he died), pointed out a partial answer to my question when he wrote,

> To put it in more modern psychological terms, most of us become desensitized or habituated to the especially delicate experiences of life. Most of us live in a world of overstimulation and sensory overload. Without realizing it, we erect defenses against our own perceptions in order to avoid being overwhelmed. We find ourselves no longer appreciative of the

> subtle sensations, delicate fragrances, soft sounds, and exquisite feelings we enjoyed as children. Like addicts experiencing *tolerance*—the need for more and more drugs to sustain their effect—many of us find ourselves seeking increasingly powerful stimulation to keep our enjoyment and satisfaction going.

He then encouraged us to recover our innocence, as well as to reestablish a new perspective and greater sensitivity, so that profound peace, exquisite joy, and the fullness of love may become possible again. But for that to happen we must stop deluding ourselves about an idea that isn't really true: that we are *already* grateful.

In addition, we need to better appreciate the connection between gratefulness and asceticism. Kathleen Norris, in her book *Dakota: A Spiritual Geography*, describes this connection quite well: "The western plains now seem bountiful in their emptiness, offering solitude to grow.... Asceticism... [is] a way of surrendering to reduced circumstances in a manner that enhances the whole person.... It may be odd to think of living in Dakota as a luxury, but I'm well aware that ours is a privileged and endangered way of life, one that ironically only the poor may be able to afford."

This statement may seem surprising at first, but when one thinks about it for a while it becomes clear. For instance, Israeli economist Avner Offer, after his survey of the impact of affluence on both developed and developing countries, comments, "Affluence breeds impatience, and impatience undermines well-being." As philosopher Søren Kierkegaard also recognized, "Most people pursue pleasure with such breathless haste that they hurry past it."

For some people, life seems such a chore that even though they have so much, they overdramatize anything negative that comes their way. It is like every third Tuesday is "dark night of the soul" day. They clearly have failed to embrace the axiom about having a healthy perspective: contentment is not the fulfillment of what you want but the realization of what you already have.

This lack of true gratefulness is partly due to a failure to realize the reality of impermanence and the danger of a habit- or anxiety-driven life. Impermanence helps us realize how pressure-filled and fleeting life can be—no matter how idyllic the setting. When I traveled to Iowa to offer a series of lectures, I had just completed a number of consultations in very difficult, urban settings. My unspoken feeling as I got on the plane was that it will be good to be in a quiet, stress-free setting again. And in one sense I was right. As I flew in over the fields of crops and wooded areas, I could feel myself decompressing. Then over dinner my host said, "I suppose it would be good for you to have a briefing on the stress we've been experiencing, since helping people deal with psychological pressures is what you do."

I must have shown surprise on my face because he smiled a bit ruefully and said, "Oh yes, it is beautiful out here in Iowa. The people have real spunk, and it is a great place to live and raise children. But even here in rural America we have had more than our share of stress recently. We have had floods that after they receded left many homes filled with mold. Following this, we had a series of brutal hailstorms that left crops flattened and destroyed. The ongoing recession has wreaked more than its share of financial woes on people who were living on so little in the first place. Finally, something quite tragic happened locally." At this point, he paused so that I could continue to absorb what he was telling me, and then added, "Our most popular high school coach was senselessly murdered. It was like we lost a favorite brother or uncle. We are still trying to make sense of this in our quiet, friendly community."

Being "in the now" and aware of the true fragility of life—namely, that we are dying and everyone else is dying too—helps us be grateful. It helps us to appreciate the people around us and the "affluence" we already possess. We begin to recognize that when we want more and get it, what do we need then? More, of course. When we believe we need something different to be happy and actually get it, what does it become then? The same, of course. And, if we believe that we need something or someone perfect to be truly happy, we run the risk of wasting our whole lives lamenting and waiting for this illusion to be realized. The reality is that when we have a truly grateful heart, everything is ours already—whether we technically own it or not.

I used to spend a lot of time working on my yard. I would be killing myself outside trying to make my property look good.

The healthy part of this was that I enjoyed the exercise and the possibilities to be creative. I also got great joy sitting in a little screened-in area looking out at the beauty of the trees, bushes, pond, and various animals that visited the property each day. It was peaceful and encouraging for living a sane life in so many ways. Yet, like all amateur landscapers, I would compare my outdoor display with the others in the neighborhood. This took some of the joy out of it and sometimes caused me to overdo it physically in an effort to produce what was just the right look.

Well, my elderly neighbor taught me a daily lesson in this regard. Each day he would pass by slowly on his walk and look over the fence and appreciate the work I had done. He would drink it in and enjoy the beauty of it all, and then walk on. He wasn't into competition or ownership. It didn't seem to matter to him whether I worked hard or not, whether it was a better display of bushes and flowers than other neighbors had or not. It didn't even appear to bother him that I temporarily held title to the land. He enjoyed it as much as I did. As a matter of fact, a lot of the time, I think he enjoyed it even more!

We miss so much of what life sets before us, and that is sad. Our minds are elsewhere on other potential possessions or desires. We miss the plate set in front of us. We are like people in a room filled with tasty Italian food, but we are busy looking for another cuisine while the food before us gets cold. Instead, if we were sensible, we would enjoy the Italian food (the present gifts in our life) before us now so we would know how to truly enjoy the other cuisines (different future gifts) later, if and when they arrived. Isn't it crazy that most of us are so concerned so much of the time about how many years we will be on this earth, but we are not even enjoying the year, month, week, day, *moment* we are living in right now?

A commitment to deep gratitude nourishes contentment by reminding us of the hidden, undeserved graces that show up each day. Most people are unfortunately oblivious to these graces because they have predetermined what will make them happy and are therefore closed to everything else that is set before them. This can happen even with respect to how we view people and interactions. It is so easy for us to narrow our perspective and fall back on prejudices based on so little information.

PERSPECTIVE, GRATEFULNESS, AND OPENNESS IN INTERPERSONAL ENCOUNTERS

For me, North Carolina represents the best of both the North and the South. I just love the Tar Heel State. It has sophisticated university cities, the ocean, the mountains, and all the rural area you would want in between. Years ago, I took a trip to the "in-between" area to speak to sheriffs on applied psychology for law enforcement officers.

As I launched into my first presentation, I was as animated as ever. I have never learned to pace myself, as some of my colleagues do. They seem to clear their desk, sit down on it, and then lecture for hours. But I find myself moving around the room, telling stories, and trying to relate principles that are practical and easy to remember.

When I present my material, I hope to engage and connect with the audience. In this case, that is just what happened…for the *most* part. While most of the men present—at the time all sheriffs in this area were male—were laughing, there was one who, through every story, no matter how rollicking it might be for the rest of the class, just sat there with a stone face. Normally this is to be expected, and it is no big deal. However, for some reason, this morning it was really getting to me, so the negative dialogue started to build within me.

"I don't have to put up with this. Here I am giving my all, and he doesn't even appreciate it. How resistant can he be? He should be up here in my place. Then he would see!" It finally got so crazy that I thought, "Well, I don't have to put up with this. After the break, I'll just give the material straight out rather than putting on such a show."

Well, the break did finally come, and the fellow I had the inner dialogue about immediately stood up straight and walked directly toward me. After he reached the podium where I was standing, he looked down at me (he was huge) and said, "I don't think you should be a teacher," and then paused. (At that moment I thought, "Didn't I have this guy pegged correctly? Am I not a great diagnostician?") He then finally broke into a youthful grin for the first time and said, "You should be an actor. That was terrific!" (And being the ethical guy that I am, I replied, "You know, I *knew* from the look on your face that you were really enjoying it.")

We predict what people are thinking and make assessments often in a negative direction without really knowing what is going on. Is it any wonder, then, that we are surprised and caught up short when the opposite is true or something other than what we expected jumps out at us?

A priest who teaches at Georgetown University told me that he was walking to school one day and encountered a homeless man asking for money. The priest decided to give him some change he had in his pocket. When he did, the man thanked him and said, "Please pray for me." The priest nodded, said he would, and then added almost as a matter of course as he was turning away, "Please pray for me too." At which point, the man said in return, "Why? What seems to be the problem?"

He hadn't expected this and started to mumble some response. At which point, the man took his hands, looked up at the sky, and prayed out loud for him for a few seconds, then let go of his hands and wished him well. Later, the priest told me he was so surprised at this because he had prejudged the man and the situation. The encounter opened "eyes of gratitude" and his outlook to seeing people and events with fewer preconceptions.

Being open and seeking *not* to be judgmental are often quite elusive undertakings, no matter how aware we try to be. Even when we think we have a sense of openness and are sensitive to what is happening around us, often we are not. We can't be, because we never have *all* the information. This is illustrated well in a classic story by Stephen Covey from his famous book *The 7 Habits of Highly Successful People*:

> One Sunday morning I was on a subway in New York. People were sitting quietly—some reading newspapers, some lost in thought, some resting with their eyes closed. It was a calm and peaceful scene.
>
> Then suddenly, a man and his children entered the subway car. The children were so loud and rambunctious that instantly the whole climate changed.
>
> The man sat down next to me and closed his eyes, apparently oblivious to the situation. The children were yelling back and forth, throwing things, even grabbing people's papers. It was very disturbing. And yet, the man sitting next to me did nothing.
>
> It was difficult not to feel irritated. I could not believe that he could be so insensitive as to let his children run wild like that and do nothing about it, taking no responsibility at all. It was easy to see that everyone else on the subway felt irritated too. So, finally, with what I felt was unusual patience and restraint, I turned to him and said, "Sir, your children are really disturbing a lot of people. I wonder if you wouldn't control them a little more?"

The man lifted his gaze as if to come to a consciousness of the situation for the first time and said softly, "Oh, you're right, I guess I should do something about it. We just came from the hospital where their mother died about an hour ago. I don't know what to think, and I guess they don't know how to handle it differently."

Can you imagine what I felt at that moment? My paradigm shifted. Suddenly I *saw* differently, I *thought* differently, I *behaved* differently. My irritation vanished. I didn't have to worry about controlling my attitude or my behavior; my heart was filled with the man's pain. Feelings of sympathy and compassion flowed freely. "Your wife just died? Oh, I'm so sorry! Can you tell me about it? What can I do to help?" Everything changed in an instant.

People are often concerned about the negative impact of their ignorance. They feel it is what they don't know that will hurt them, and this of course is true, to a certain extent. However, I believe that an even more subtle, insidious danger than ignorance is that which we think we already know but actually don't. True sensitivity and real wisdom at the core of a healthy perspective begin with recognizing this fact by minding our predictions or evaluations of others.

At times we tend to be so hard-hearted that even when presented with contrary information, we "dig in our heels" and hold onto our opinions rather than being open enough to let in new information that may prove us wrong. I think the following humorous story shared by psychologist and spiritual writer Anthony de Mello illustrates this point well:

> A woman suddenly stops a man walking down the street and says, "Henry, I am so happy to see you after all these years! My, how you have changed. I remember you as being tall, and you seem so much shorter now. You used to have a pale complexion, and it is really so ruddy now. Good grief, how you have changed in five years!"
>
> Finally, the man gets a chance to interject, "But my name isn't Henry!"
>
> To which the persistent woman calmly responds, "Oh, so you changed your name too!"

As Emmons has noted in his book *Thanks!*, gratitude is an attitude that has many worthy ideas and aspects (see Box 8). To be aware of them is a way of honoring both the importance and difficulty of being a grateful person in a sometimes entitlement-driven society. If we wish to be grateful people, then we need to make the effort to enhance our perspective in a way that allows us to open ourselves to what is *already* in our lives. To do this, we must face the fear that gratitude for what we have already is tantamount to settling for life as it is now and not being open to receiving or seeking more. True gratitude is also an essential cornerstone of happiness, an equally important subject worth pursuing to gain and maintain a healthier perspective.

Box 8 Helpful Ideas on Understanding and Enhancing Gratitude

The following are a number of ideas put forth by Robert Emmons in his book *Thanks!* and other authors/sources on this topic; they are refocused and summarized here with an eye to their significance in the process of enhancing a healthy attitude toward, and perspective on, self and life.

- Gratitude seems simple, but it is quite a complex phenomenon. You can view it as an emotion, an attitude, or a way of living. When seeking to gain a healthy perspective, it becomes a crucial part of ensuring you don't miss what you have been given, and opens your eyes to what else might come your way—albeit in "small" packages that reflect how the prevailing society might label them.
- Sometimes people avoid gratitude because they fear that expressing thanks may then make them beholden to others. Because they experienced neediness early in life, they also fear that others won't recognize their difficulties if they seem grateful for what they have gotten. The result is a decrease in the likelihood of receiving the positive emotional, mental, physical, spiritual, relational, and societal consequences opened by gratitude.
- Gratitude, as in the case of mindfulness, requires practice. Setting gratitude in place during meditation doesn't mean avoiding or diminishing the losses or negative events in

life; it does mean that any support from within or without can be maximized.

- Like resilience, people have a set range or "set-point" for gratitude; through practice, however, that range can be maximized.
- Gratitude is emphasized as a key virtue in many religions and spiritual practices. These frameworks encourage consistent and regular offerings of gratitude through activities such as prayer and service to others.
- Gratitude is not only for the good times. In fact, gratitude takes on a depth in "dark times" that provides comfort. (A student of mine, whose younger brother fell into a deep crevasse and died in Alaska during a school trip, was impressed by the wonderful support she received from people in her community that she didn't even know; she learned the difference that friendship and support can make during very tough times.)
- Activities that support a grateful attitude (writing emails of appreciation, journaling grateful moments, or texting inspirational messages to friends) can be helpful reminders and excellent enhancements of an attitude of thankfulness that will then lead to a healthier perspective on self and life. (Practicing gratitude through activities is also tantamount to recognizing that having this attitude is not easy; a life of gratitude can easily be replaced by one centered on entitlement and disappointment about what we *don't* have.)

(*continued*)

Box 8 (Continued)

- Gratitude helps people gain a healthier perspective by getting out of themselves; being focused inordinately on self does not lead to greater happiness, although the purpose may be this. Instead, over-self-involvement can lead to cognitive distortions and unhealthy aspects of narcissism.
- Finally, in Emmons own words, "By appreciating the gifts of the moment, gratitude frees us from past regrets and future anxieties. By cultivating gratefulness, we are freed from envy over what we don't have or who we are not. It doesn't make life perfect, but with gratitude comes the realization that right now, in this moment, we have enough, we are enough." In other words, in this moment, we have the healthiest perspective possible: we have the psychological pearl of great price.

HAPPINESS

Some people seem naturally happy. Scientist and Buddhist scholar Matthieu Ricard doesn't dispute this, but in his book *Happiness* he indicates that, like gratitude, happiness is an attitude that must be nurtured by all of us—no matter whether we tend to be happy or not: "I have... met human beings who were enduringly happy. More, in fact, than what we usually call happy: they were inbred with a deep insight into the reality and the nature of mind, and filled with benevolence for others. I have also come to understand that although some people are naturally happier than others, this happiness as a way of being, is a skill."

As in the case of gratitude, because of our constitutional nature or other factors, we may be predisposed to being happy; however, each of us can maximize our range of potential happiness.

The benefits of happiness extend beyond just the enjoyment of good feelings. In fact, research indicates that joy pays major physical and psychological dividends. Compared to their dour counterparts, as Seligman points out in his book *Authentic Happiness,* happy people

- are healthier and live longer;
- are more productive at work and have higher incomes;
- are more tolerant and creative, and make decisions more easily;
- select more challenging goals, persist longer, and perform better in a variety of laboratory tasks; and
- demonstrate greater empathy, have close friends, and enjoy better marriages.

Psychologist Barbara Frederickson has also found a relationship between positive emotions and joy. Positive emotions enable individuals to build a variety of personal resources, including physical (skills, health, longevity), social (friendships, social support networks), intellectual (expert knowledge, intellectual complexity), and psychological (resilience, optimism, creativity) resources. Her theory emphasizes that positive emotions strengthen resources that are drawn on throughout life to improve coping and improve our odds of survival. Moreover, happiness is a cornerstone of true compassion toward others. In the words of Robert Louis Stevenson, "There is no duty we so underrate as the duty to be happy. By being happy we sow anonymous benefits upon the world."

As in the case of gratitude, happiness is obviously not something that is simply wished into reality. It helps to read the works of those who have studied it, like Ricard and Seligman. In addition, we need to embrace guidance on how to develop ways to enhance a personal sense of happiness and optimism (see Box 9). Practices and careful approaches to developing stronger positive outlooks can make all the difference. (The list of questions provided at the end of this chapter is longer than in the other chapters as part of this recommended practice.)

The point here is that flourishing in life, which requires a healthy perspective, takes effort. And as Walker Percy in his book *The Moviegoer* notes, life should be a pilgrimage or search: "The search is what anyone would understand if he were not sunk in the everydayness of his own life....To become aware of the possibility of the search is to be onto something. Not to be onto something is to be in despair."

Box 9 Enhancing Happiness and Optimism

The following simple suggestions are made in accordance with positive psychology research. By taking or reinforcing the following actions, you can strengthen your own sense of well-being, quality of life, and happiness in an array of ways that in turn will enhance resilience.

1. Take stock of your gifts and talents in equal proportion to your shortcomings and the growing edges you may have in your personal life and at work. Should negativity intrude, set it aside or consider what a wise friend may say about your talents. Such an exercise can lead to healthy optimism as well as a clearer awareness of the strengths you have and can bring to bear on a myriad of personal and occupational situations.
2. Become involved in leisure activities that require interactions with others. This will meet natural needs for community and service, provide stimulation, and may involve all-consuming activities that will produce a sense of *flow* as well as require use of personal talents. When such elements as music and altruism are also present, these leisure experiences may be even more powerful since they provide aesthetic moments and a reinforcement of your value system that can positively affect your level of happiness. Likewise, you will also find that investing intentionally in community will enrich and focus your alonetime.

(*continued*)

Box 9 (Continued)

3. Although shopping can be fun and earning a good salary is rewarding, wanting more (material goods, fame, etc.) and getting it promote a natural desire to acquire even more. This in turn fosters more of the same. Likewise, seeking the so-called perfect in life, which will supposedly provide security and happiness, will eventually lead us to the realization that we have missed what life has already granted us. But by placing greater emphasis on life's free, abundant gifts, we improve our quality of life exponentially and can become a resilient, helpful presence to others. (Research shows that after we earn a salary that meets our basic needs, additional money does little—if anything!—to improve our quality of life. Remembering this simple proven fact can immeasurably reduce stress, increase happiness, and prevent inner resilience from being eroded by a future "purchase" of joy that always seems to elude us.)
4. Enhance gratefulness by remembering to compare yourself to others less fortunate, instead of focusing only on those who seem to have more than you do. This will lessen negative feelings and allow you to focus more on what you already have, thus enabling you to enjoy it even more. Those of us in health care know that even taking a walk or breathing without pain is a pure gift that we often take for granted. (Hold your breath for a while, and you will

certainly become grateful for the simple ability to breathe the air around you.)

5. From your exercises in gratitude, take note of the rewarding elements in all aspects of your life. Start with the people, activities, and things that you obviously enjoy: your spouse, someone at work who makes you laugh, the quiet few moments you spend in the morning over tea, or when you first get into work before others arrive. These elements often provide simple, unnoticed moments of joy. Why let them remain that way? See how you might take them less for granted.
6. Instead of filling your evening hours by watching television or surfing the Internet, develop some interactive hobbies or activities. These tend to renew us much more than passively sitting in front of a screen.
7. Shift out of yourself more often through service activities such as taking an elderly neighbor to the pharmacy or serving breakfast to the homeless. Reaching out can bring with it a sense of happiness that other self-oriented activities will rarely provide.
8. Learn to intentionally enjoy life and your relationships more. Instead of running through life, pause. Whether you're looking at photos taken by a friend or relative, enjoying a note from a daughter or grandson, or gratefully recalling an experience or deed that turned a good day into one filled with fun or joy, the goal is to appreciate

(*continued*)

Box 9 (Continued)

the many gifts now present. (People who can't savor are always searching for more or what they can't have rather than fully enjoying what is already within their reach.)

9. Seek to be a happy explorer in life in little and large ways. As Carr notes in his fine 2004 work *Positive Psychology: The Science of Happiness and Human Strengths*, "Evidence from developmental and laboratory studies show that positive mood states help people build enduring personal resources. Developmental studies of securely and insecurely attached children show that the former exhibit greater persistence, flexibility and resourcefulness in solving problems than the latter. They also show greater exploratory behavior in novel situations and develop superior cognitive maps [ways of understanding what they are experiencing]. Adults with secure attachment styles are more curious and open to new information than those with insecure attachment styles. Educational studies of children show that children in positive mood states learn faster.... In view of [the] evidence which shows that positive emotions can [also] facilitate creativity and problem solving, it is not surprising that happiness also increases work productivity."
10. Savor more of your life: slow down and attend to what you are eating and drinking; share a compliment you

receive by emailing it a friend; flow with and relish what you are working on; thoroughly enjoy the good times with family and friends; lean back and marvel over something you have learned…or unlearned; take photos of places you visit, but also enjoy the sites while you are there and *then* also take the time to enjoy the photos later; take a real breath during your myriad journeys, such as when you walk to get a cup of tea or visit someone. (Someone once said that life is something that happens while we are busy doing something else; taking time to note and being mindful can make the day richer and bring clarity and crispness to your perspective.)

11. Don't repress a smile or a laugh: enjoy feeling and expressing these positive and enjoyable expressions.
12. Own and fully value your talents and gifts (analytic ability, humor, caring concern, attention to detail, facility to be able to vision, etc.), and share them freely with others at times and in ways that they can be received most beneficially.
13. Spend more time being intrigued about yourself and others by refraining from or, at the very least, catching yourself when there is a tendency to project blame, condemn yourself, or become discouraged because of preconceived expectations.

SOME QUESTIONS TO CONSIDER AT THIS POINT . . .

Because exercise induces positive moods in the short term, do you take at least a short walk each day as a minimum form of exercise?

Do you truly believe that an attitude of happiness allows you to enjoy everything that is already in your life and that unhealthy attachment or clinging, on the other hand, leads to unhappiness?

Do you believe that certain things or people cause your happiness and without them you have no choice but to be miserable no matter who/what else is in your life?

Unfinished business (memories of rebuffs, trauma, the unfairness of life, etc.) tie us to the past and can be habit-forming. Do you seek to shed those chains by focusing on the gifts in your life now so the habit of looking back in sorrow, with anger or guilt, doesn't deprive you of enjoying what you have been given?

Studies have shown that positive emotions such as joy and contentment broaden the creative flexible way we think, adapt, and act as well as help us build resources that can be tapped when life gets tough. They also help us "get out of ourselves" and increase our community involvement. Think of your own positive emotions and ask, "What have they done for me?"

You can immediately improve your "gratefulness history" by reviewing your past and improving your awareness of all you have received. Take a few moments and write down a cursory review of them; how does seeing them "in print" make you feel? (Suggestion: Do this more in depth, and send off an email or brief note to some of the people to whom you feel you should offer thanks.)

Savoring life is one of the actions we can do to enhance both gratitude and happiness. How do you undertake this each day informally and intentionally at times? (Suggestion: Because this helps us appreciate more fully all that is and has been in our lives, it is good to "revisit" friends and possessions [home, car, favorite room, food or activity] and make believe you are seeing/experiencing them again for the first time.)

What is an activity that you lose yourself in that you dearly love/are stimulated by/have fun with? (Csikszentmihalyi called this "flow.")

How and when has your sense of both gratitude and happiness encouraged you to "pay it forward" by sharing with others—not out of guilt or duty but naturally, with no expectations of anything (even a smile or thank-you) in return?

Seeking immediate satisfaction through the use of drugs, avoiding a challenge you need to face, or exacting revenge may lead to initial pleasure but not to ultimate happiness. How do you distinguish between these experiences and their different consequences?

Having different (prophetic, encouraging, humorous, and inspirational) voices to listen to in our interpersonal network helps us keep a healthy perspective with gratitude and happiness as fruits. Where are these types of friends in your life?[1]

Do you enhance/expand friendship in your life by being faithful in your promises; volunteering; being flexible and tolerant; having a sense of

---

[1] In the book *Bounce: Living the Resilient Life,* I have dealt more extensively in describing these four "voices" or types of friends.

humor; receiving people's stories of success and failure with interest and support; being encouraging and interested in their welfare; and being grateful for their presence in your life?

How do you ensure you don't hear praise in a whisper and negative feedback as thunder?

Do you catch yourself when you are comparing who you are and what you have with those who seem to have more than you do?

What are you committed to in life that provides you with the greatest long-term satisfaction?

Where do you find meaning in your life? Because this element can enhance your overall happiness, how do you get greater clarity around the importance and different aspects that meaning offers? How can you involve yourself more deeply or frequently in activities that enhance this sense of meaning?

How do you discern between real physical, psychological, and spiritual needs for your happiness, peace, and joy in life and those that are only desirable but not necessary so you don't feel unnecessarily impoverished?

What areas of your life are fun, and how can you allot more time to them rather than continually postponing them until "after" (you graduate, get a job, get promoted, get married, have children, your children are grown, retire, etc.)?

Do you consider yourself an optimistic and hopeful person? If so, why? If not, given the previous questions and the material in the previous chapters, what practices might foster a healthier perspective that would reap more optimism and hope as its fruits?

What are some of the key elements (e.g., enjoying beauty, maintaining good relationships, having an opportunity to use your talents and skills, involving yourself in relaxing and renewing activities, improving your intellectual abilities, satisfying your creative impulses) that contribute to the quality in your life? How might you structure your life to increase their presence and predominance in ways that not only allow you to flourish but also benefit those who interact with you?

FOUR

Seeing in the Darkness

Appreciating the Paradox of Posttraumatic Growth

Compassion for ourselves arises in the practice of opening to our own suffering. The mere presence of suffering is not enough. Consider how easy it is to become hardened by devastating loss or hardship. Mindfulness offers a way to change our relationship to suffering by surrendering our need to reject it. This is an act of kindness to oneself. Our own suffering offers an opportunity to become openhearted rather than merely oppressed.

Paul Fulton, *Mindfulness and Psychotherapy*

At home that night I thought of the suffering he had endured. It had stripped him of all that was false.

George Crane, *Bones of the Master*

What happens when we are standing in the darkness and clarity is fugitive? What does a healthier perspective look like then? People who have experienced physical violence, sexual terror, and psychological or spiritual abuse must confront these hard questions. But all of us walk down life's dark hallways at times. Unexpected loss, a surprising illness or divorce, drug abuse by our siblings or children, loss of employment (and possibly for some of us, our identity) all make up the interpersonal landscapes of life, *your* life at times.

No one escapes personal darkness. Yet our perspective (once again, *how* we perceive life) can make all the difference in where it ultimately leads for us and those whose lives are eventually touched by us. Significant loss, unwanted change, trauma, and serious illness befall all of us at some point. And we are usually caught off guard. It is hard to believe that something so awful has happened to *us*! We may also be surprised by our overwhelming response to such trauma or serious stress. As one young man shared with me after experiencing a sense of deep grief, "I had no idea my body could hold so much sadness."

Fear also is a common companion to sadness whenever significant unwanted change occurs. Author bell hooks captures this reality well in her memoir *All about Love*:

> My grief was a heavy, despairing sadness caused by parting from a companion of many years but, more important, it was a despair rooted in the fear that love did not exist, could not be found. And even if it were lurking somewhere, I might never know it in my lifetime. It had become hard for me to continue to believe in love's promise when everywhere I turned the enchantment of power or the terror of fear overshadowed the will to love.

Negative changes are certainly unwanted and should not be denied for what they are: *terrible*. However, as all of us realize at some level, unfortunately, they are part of life. Still, although the trauma and stresses everyone must experience at times are certainly undesirable, fairly recent psychological research on posttraumatic *growth* (PTG) now shows what classic wisdom has intuited for generations—namely, unwanted painful events can actually take people to growthful places in themselves and life that would not have been possible *if* they *hadn't* had the terrible encounters in the first place and also had the wherewithal to see and embrace the promises such experiences had to offer. With this in mind, here are some essential questions to ask:

What does it take for people to shift their perspective so that they can respond to significant stress and trauma in ways that deepen their self-understanding and compassion toward themselves and others?

What does it take for these negative events to actually provide benefit rather than leading only to numbness and bitterness or, at best, return them to a pre-upheaval level of functioning?

Almost in response to these questions, two movements have occurred in the behavioral sciences. One, *positive psychology* (discussed in Chapter 2), has given life to an area being referred to now as "posttraumatic growth," which points to the ways suffering can lead to amazingly fortunate results. The other, *mindfulness* (discussed in Chapter 1), has been put forth by a number of psychotherapeutic schools of thought (including cognitive behavioral therapy and acceptance and commitment therapy) as a way of becoming present in order to diminish anxiety and enhance the quality of life.

These two psychological advances are even more fascinating because they complement and build on each other, as well as provide empirical evidence and new angles of vision, with respect to the classic and contemporary wisdom literature from philosophy, spirituality, and humanistic-existential psychology that predated them. In the past, as most will now acknowledge, clinical psychology was so pathology-driven and in line with the medical model that it viewed the challenges people faced in life as "acute." In other words, the goal was to find out what was causing the problem, fix it, and then move on (although, as David Brazier in his important work *Zen Therapy* aptly noted, it was often a return to what Freud referred to as a stage of "ordinary unhappiness").

But some people, such as existentialists and Buddhists, and other world spiritualities (Jewish, Christian, Muslim, Hindu) had a seemingly opposite approach. They saw life as "chronic." Consequently, they were more interested *not* so much in eliminating or running away from life's problems (as if addressed, they all could actually be solved anyway) as they were in greeting each day in ways in which *all* of life, including—maybe *especially*—pain and suffering, were faced mindfully and thus beneficially. If we wish to have a healthy perspective and lead the fullest life possible, given the realities in life, when we encounter personal darkness, are facing suffering, or are seeking to walk with those in our interpersonal network who have experienced trauma or great stress we must seek to do it mindfully.

As Germer points out in *Mindfulness and Psychotherapy*, Buddhist psychology teaches us that the patient "may be seeking freedom *from* her anxiety, but as therapy progresses, [the patient] actually discovers freedom in her anxiety. How does this occur? A strong therapeutic alliance may encourage [the patient] to explore her panic more closely.... The patient discovers that he or she need not avoid the experience to feel better."

Once, a young Catholic priest from New Zealand learned this lesson during his first year out of the seminary. I asked him a question I ask of all clinical psychologists, counselors, social workers, psychiatrists, nurses, chaplains, educators, physicians, and persons in full-time ministry after they have been out of training for a while, namely, "Since completion of your courses and field work, is there a certain interaction that stands out for you as a memorable learning experience?" In response, the priest shared what he felt was his most teachable moment in the year since his ordination:

> I received a message that I was needed at the hospital, but the young person who took the message failed to also leave the name of the individual requesting my visit. Since the hospital was a small one, I decided to visit there anyway to see if I could find out who called for me. When I entered the lobby of the hospital I could see a distressed couple in the corner: he was crying, and she looked desolate.
>
> I took a chance, walked over, introduced myself, and asked if they had called for a priest to visit. They nodded and told me that it was they who had called. They then explained that they had just given birth to twins and one was born alive but the other was born dead.

"What did you do then?" I asked.

> We then went down into the morgue and stood around the little figure covered by a shroud and we prayed and we cried.
>
> Then, almost like a resurrection experience, we went up the stairs to the neonatal intensive care unit to visit the other child. When we entered the unit, it was a totally different experience. Unlike the morgue, there was real life there. The walls were brightly painted, mobiles hung from the ceiling, and there was a lot of chatter and energy. We then stood around the incubator and prayed and cried again—but this time, they were tears of joy.

Then after a pause, the priest added,

> The lesson for me in this poignant encounter was: I don't think I would have been able to cry those tears of joy if I hadn't first cried those tears of sadness. Sometimes, for good things to be experienced, I must also be willing to face directly those which don't feel good at all.

Once again, when posttraumatic growth occurs, we begin to appreciate that it is not the amount of darkness in the world that matters. It is not even the amount of darkness in ourselves that matters. In the end, it is how we stand in that darkness that is of the essence.

There is a Zen proverb, which I think other world spiritualities would support, that gently suggests, "If you relax and make yourself comfortable, you can journey anywhere." And so, for posttraumatic growth to occur and be reinforced, this is exactly what we must seek to do. Openness is related to growth, and possessing and enhancing this personality trait within ourselves and others increases the likelihood for growth.

In psychological darkness caused by trauma and serious stress, people may embrace humility as they see how little they control in life and how much is overlooked, or never unwrapped, in their lives. This recognition is crucial because when humility is added to the knowledge gained during a dark period in life, it can then become new wisdom. And when you add this very wisdom to compassion, it has an opportunity to become selfless love. And so, even though the PTG literature does not directly support this hypothesis, I believe we must at least consider this possibility concerning humility when reflecting on and moving ahead in our own lives—especially during difficult times.

Posttraumatic growth also teaches us that when there is true acceptance of the reality and tragedy of a traumatic loss, there is often a recognition that we would still trade *all* of our post-traumatic growth if we could miraculously undo the cause of the trauma. However, if we have had to face some overwhelming, unexpected stress, obviously uncovering formerly unexpressed mindfulness, perspective, gratitude, happiness, freedom, creativity, courage, forgiveness, acceptance, patience, openness, and *hope* is, of course, desirable.

Renowned UK and American publisher Harold Evans recalls an interaction with his daughter in his memoir *Paper Chase*:

> Around the time of 9/11, Isabel, then eleven, was asked at school whether she was British or American. She said she was "Amerikish." Some months after 9/11 her homework for a class in Greek mythology was to make a Pandora's box. We asked her what she'd put in it. She showed us an empty plate for hunger, a Tylenol bottle for disease, a cracked mirror for vanity, and a chocolate for greed. There was also a tiny colored drawing she had made of the Stars and Stripes.
>
> "And that?" we asked.
>
> "Hope," she said.
>
> I often think of that today.

Again, a key question is, are we in tune with both the potential appearances and ways of enhancing posttraumatic growth that leads to new hope?

The road to recovery and possible new growth may be a very long one. Patience is the sibling of courage in the journey toward gaining a new perspective and growth. If we are to be mindful, we need to recognize this with respect to ourselves as well as others.

Being patient when we experience trauma or encounter severe stress, personal loss, or hurt is not easy, though. We may initially want quick change, improvement, or a solution, as may our family and circle of friends who may also push us to move forward. This desire for us to improve or somehow become "fixed" or cured is a natural one. After all, who wants to be in an unpleasant place in life? The difference hinges on gaining new insights through patience and pacing recovery to meet our internal needs versus the needs of others around us.

For instance, a friend of mine had been sexually abused as a child and had all but repressed this reality. Later on in life she started to become aware of it and became depressed. During therapy, she reported to the counselor that despite her dark outlook, each morning she would get up and go down to have breakfast and a morning chat with those she lived with: "I only did this because I didn't want them to know I was feeling so badly." To which the therapist responded, "You may feel that now since you are depressed, but the other perspective is that you are able to get out of bed and interact despite how you feel. Others who are depressed may not able to do this; *you* are. Given this, please make a list of any other positive actions—no matter how you view the real reasons you have for doing them—so we can see them more clearly for what they are: *acts of courage*."

In responding this way, my friend was able to eventually see how she was erroneously casting away her meaningful actions in a dismissive fashion. When we are able to be patient and focus, we help both ourselves and others who are under great stress to become more aware of the progress that is present amidst the gray, depressive outlook that follows trauma. This patient attention to greater clarity can better open the door to new revelations. Often people miss these acts of courage or play down their significance, but the decrease in fear and willingness to directly deal with this trauma is just that: an act of courage.

Yet, for this to happen, it helps if we have patience for our or their growth—whether we have experienced a terrible tragedy in our lives or not. In the words of Ernest Hemingway in his classic work *A Moveable Feast,* "When the cold rains kept on and killed the spring, it was as though a young person had died for no reason. In those days, though, the spring always came finally; but it was frightening that it had nearly failed." In our own lives, and in being a calm presence within the stormy lives of others, we must remind ourselves, in a gentle, persistent way, as Thomas Merton did for a discouraged brother: "*Courage comes and goes. Hold on for the next supply.*"

FROM ASSUMING PERMANENCE IN LIFE TO ACCEPTING THE REALITY OF IMPERMANENCE

No one likes personal darkness. Nor should we. But as I have noted earlier, at times there is just no way around it. Yet the option lies for us in *how* we respond to ours and others' trauma, severe loss, great crises, and deep sadness, and to the unfolding of past and new narratives.

As we know from simply looking around in today's world, darkness crushes and embitters some people. Others may seek to ignore the impact of the trauma, hoping it will just eventually go away—which it rarely does. Or they—often with the help of a healthy, informed therapeutic presence in their life—may persistently (but at times not patiently) face the trauma and severe stress clearly and compassionately so it can soften and teach them—and *us* if we are standing with them in the darkness—new lessons in living. As Viktor Frankl, psychiatrist and Holocaust survivor reminds us, "Everything can be taken from a person but one thing: the last of the human freedoms—to choose one's attitude in any given set of circumstances, to choose one's own way."

These lessons learned as a result of trauma may not return us or others to where we or they were before the darkness descended: nothing can do that. Yet the literature that is building on posttraumatic growth shows that with time, reflection, support, hard work, and openness, we and others may in fact be led to places within ourselves that would never have been reached had the trauma not occurred in the first place. There is no magic in this. As a matter of fact, it begins to a great extent with the acceptance of an important reality, that an *irreversible change* has occurred: a loved one has died or been killed, someone has been abused or raped, a childhood has been taken away, someone has suffered an unwanted divorce or job loss, war atrocities have been witnessed or committed, a reputation has been forever ruined.

Again, there has been a permanent change to us or others in the community. Nothing can alter that. Yet, to all of us interested in PTG, the obvious, valuable question in the fore then—with no preordained answer, psychological route, or time frame because each person and situation is unique—is, *now what?*

Through the use of "alonetime," or our own mindfulness meditation practice, that includes an openness to the fragility of life and a sense of the reality of impermanence as well as a knowledge of the possibility of PTG, we become willing and prepare to sit with ourselves and others who are confronting the reality of having encountered an irreversible unwanted change in our or their lives. When we are aware of the recognition that birth always ends in death, gathering with releasing, and meeting with departing, life may then be freer, and we will have greater "space" within, to be more compassionate with ourselves and others. We will also taste life's gifts more completely because we will no longer be tempted to take them for granted.

FROM SELF-CENTEREDNESS TO ACCEPTANCE AND COMPASSION

Initially, when a crisis or trauma occurs, we and others tend to pull inward for protection. In the beginning, that's natural and good. People who have experienced trauma can't take too much outside stimuli. They need room to acknowledge, grieve, adjust, let go... *survive.* They must keep to themselves and heal. They need time to come to terms with all that has occurred and the changes that have taken place in what they assumed about themselves and the world—even when everything continues to move forward and appear "normal."

We see this reflected in the African memoir of Alexandra Fuller (*Cocktail Hour under the Tree of Forgetfulness*) when she quotes her mother, who has just lost one of her very young children to illness: "I remember walking out of the hospital and being so shocked that the world was still there. All the jacarandas were in blossom. Salisbury looked so beautiful. The flower sellers were in Meikles Park, the agapanthus were out, the jasmine was so sweet. And I thought, 'How can the world look normal? How can everyone not understand that the world has come to an end?'"

Yet, at some point, serious stress or trauma survivors must look externally to continue to move beyond survival. Otherwise, the ironic result in focusing solely on the loss, trauma, crisis, or perpetrator will be to chain oneself unconsciously to the pain. At some point, for growth to become possible and blossom, there must be a letting go or, more appropriately, *a living with* the unwanted experience or trauma in a new way.

For instance, some of the Tibetan monks who were tortured by their jailors in Chinese prisons recognized this to an incredible degree. One even said to the Dalai Lama after his escape that he was "afraid that one day he might lose his sympathy for his Chinese captors." Quite amazing.

However, as noted earlier, for natural, deep compassion—not driven by an attitude based on duty or guilt—to be rich for trauma victims as well as those who walk with them, healthy self-centeredness (appropriate self-care/understanding/love) is initially necessary. Once this takes root and there are signs that new growth is present (conversations are not as focused on what happened in the past but are more present/future-focused and the person seems more empowered than self-defining him/herself as a victim), then compassionate action on his/her part becomes a significant aspect in the movement toward integrating growth.

It may begin, for instance, with safely expressing anger at situations in which others have been traumatized. At a certain juncture later in the process, when a fuller acceptance of what has happened starts to lead to new personal growth and depth, a wider interest in others may start to evidence itself in other more concrete ways. (Persons or survivor groups that stay focused on themselves forever and don't eventually look out of themselves with compassion may be an indication that PTG might not take place for them.)

Returning to the example of the Tibetan monks who were tortured, not all of them felt as much benevolence as the monk mentioned earlier. In one instance, provided by psychologist Jack Kornfield, an elder monk asked a younger one if he felt compassion now toward his former captors. The younger man answered vehemently, "Never!" to which the more senior monk softly responded, "Well, they still have you in prison then, don't they?"

Following trauma or a very negative event, a person has the choice to take either fork in the road: continue forever on the road of bitterness, regret, anger, and depression; or, when the timing is right and if the person is emotionally able, take another more freeing route—new growth, wisdom, freedom, and compassion.

THE MINDFUL PERSON AND TRAUMA

When we are mindful by being in the now, aware, and open, the stage is set for increasing the possibility of growth by taking the more beneficial path following trauma and stress. So, when we are in this place, and are wise (and therefore well aware of personal limitations—that is, have a degree of true humility), we can then appreciate the need to do the following:

- Honor life's fragility.
- Be mindful to facilitate a greater appreciation for and participation in life which will promote greater learning.
- Let go of the "whys" and experience the now, not just cognitively, but emotionally and spiritually.
- Practice self-compassion: maintain a personal self-care regimen and healing rituals. For those poised for growth, this is not simply a psychological duty but a natural expression of the full self.
- Recognize that we surprisingly make war with ourselves because of a desire to control the uncontrollable in ourselves and our interactions with others.

- Appreciate the value of simplicity in how we both view and live life, while having an intentional approach to seeking periods of silence and solitude for reflection and mindfulness.
- Embrace a willingness to face our own *koans* (life puzzles) that have no easy answers but require choices that will affect our lives.
- See the differences between "pain" (what happens to us) and "suffering" (the negative results that arise from the perspective we either unconsciously or consciously have toward this painful event).

With such fruits of personal maturity as these (and the many others that may come from a sense of mindfulness and personal awareness), we further enhance the process of PTG when its seeds start to break the surface of our lives. We see more clearly so that we can in turn guide others to appreciate the following (if and when we and they might be open to these life realities):

- Realize that a current basic set of assumptions will not always work—life changes, and so must our outlook.
- Appreciate that loss of control, meaning, and predictability will occur at times; how we perceive these and respond accordingly is the key to personal growth and depth.
- Understand that although no one wants trauma, pain, and sadness, they can teach us new lifelong lessons... *if* we are open to letting them.

- Acknowledge that perspective and priorities that change in response to experiencing trauma can alter one's philosophy of life in unforeseen, rewarding ways by providing a richer narrative about one's own personal life.
- Become open to and aware of the process of others' growth, with no preconceived expectations or need for them to undergo the experience. One of the best ways for us to prepare for this is to use the same reflective approach to growth in ourselves during periods of "alonetime" in silence, solitude, and mindful meditation.
- Welcome the appearance of new positive meaning making after trauma as something filled with potential rather than simply a form of resistance or denial. (This is so when there is *also* a full recognition of the adverse nature of the event present; positive meaning making is not real if there is a denial or a downplaying of the reality that something terrible in fact has happened.)
- Appreciate the value of sometimes underrated personality traits of "curiosity" and "openness" that play a significant role in determining whether growth is possible.
- Explore the role of openness to forgiveness and compassion (as distinct from reconciliation or forgetting) when the timing is right.
- Appreciate that psychological researchers have presented studies on growth after trauma, but that there is much nonempirical "wisdom literature" that predates this (such as works by Frankl and Yalom, as well as mindfulness and

spiritual approaches to suffering that are both theistic and nontheistic such as Buddhism) and that learning widely and deeply about PTG could expand our access to it and benefit us personally, as well as enrich others walking this path.

- Appreciate that PTG is *not* based simply on a positive reframing of a negative event but a *simultaneous* honoring the undesirability/horror of it while being open to possibly unforeseeable growth that might not have occurred had the significant stress or traumatic event not happened.
- Discern between the perception of the distress experienced by us (or people we interact with) and the severity of the trauma itself since the *former* is actually of greater import in terms of impact. Our perspective on trauma or serious stress is the key.
- Fathom the importance of our perspective when we become upset at the possibility that we seem to have lost our way in life. Daniel Boone was once asked whether, given his tracking skills, he had ever gotten lost. He answered, "No. But I was bewildered once for three days."
- Acknowledge the subtle, yet crucial, roles that patience and pacing play in supporting others and ourselves on the journey toward PTG since stress is part of being human. The lesson? Be gentle, and give yourself and others plenty of time to adjust, heal, and deepen.
- Appreciate the potential for faith, religious community, image of god, spiritual strength, and other related religious

themes in your own or other people's journey after great stress has occurred because they can be either a deterrent or enhancement to the growth process.

- Discern the difference between the early, naturally occurring, constructive ruminations, which help us adjust by realizing and incorporating what has happened, and the deliberate and negative ones, which are intrusive. After trauma, ruminations that appear immediately are often natural and may lead to growth, whereas thoughts that become obsessive and remain long after the trauma may not.

MEANING MAKING

Given all of these guides, at the heart of an openness to growth after trauma is an understanding of the reality that, after the jolt created by the trauma, loss, or significant stress to our psychological system, new meaning making must occur as well. The groundbreaking work of such researchers as Crystal Park and Robert A. Neimeyer has helped us immeasurably in understanding this process.

Psychological research on coping articulates that when a person experiences a trauma, the usual approaches to problem solving are not sufficient to decrease the person's sense of distress. After all, you can't "solve" a rape, the death of a child, or a sudden job loss or divorce. What is needed is assistance in the search for new meaning in life.

Meaning making is more than putting a positive cast on something. It involves attributing global meaning (the way we view life)—what we consider fair (young people do not die), what we thought we had control over, and how we predict things. It also involves attributing situational meaning—the meaning we assign to specific life events.

What often happens is that these two processes collide after a tragic event and then the person is left to deal with the disparity and dissonance. For instance, an innocent child may die in a terrible storm. Our global meaning may tell us that bad things shouldn't happen to little children, whereas our situational meaning accounts for these things happening in nature.

After such a tragedy, some people remain upset because they cannot reconcile the two (global and situational) types of meaning. Others change their situational or global meaning to accommodate the other so they can reach a new, possibly deeper place for themselves and what life offers. When this happens, people view themselves, events, others, their values, sense of meaning, and relationships differently. They also may develop new ways of living, coping, relating, as well as a more satisfying attitude toward life that allows them to value the moment, other people, and the little things in life as never before.

This happens when people often tentatively entertain new beliefs as a bridge to a healthier perspective on life. This is so especially when these new assumptions don't avoid or deny something unpleasant, but rather serve as a means of being open in new ways that weren't present—or even possible!—in the past.

These initial steps of making sense out of the new normal are like being handed life's menu again. The hope is that we won't simply lament that our former favorites are no longer there. Instead, it urges us to try new selections with an openness that doesn't deny the absence or loss of something or someone we loved before, but does tentatively explore potentially new joys.

At times, finding new meaning/assumptions about our lives will be difficult or impossible. This isn't terrible. It is just the reality under certain circumstances. The process of meaning making, though, as was indicated above, helps us and others adopt new assumptions about life that eventually will provide enough closure after the trauma or loss so new ways of seeing and experiencing life, *our* lives, become possible.

Posttraumatic growth occurs after an experience of trauma, great stress, or personal darkness, when a new perspective arises and helps us realize something previously unencountered in the way we view life. We acknowledge the experience, without denying the sadness or personal horror of it, but are open to seeing something new. The new sense is, "I thought my life was a dark house in which I was locked. Now I see it was only a dark hallway, and I have opened the door now to a new series of healthy perspectives on the present and future, which gives me a life I could never have dreamed of before."

FINAL COMMENTS

Each person, due to differences in personality, history, support, and faith experience, among other things, will respond to severe sudden stress and trauma in different ways. That is to be expected. However, *knowledge about and readiness to experience the possibility of PTG* can make all the difference in capitalizing on these events in our lives and in those close to us.

The essential question we confronted briefly here is, will the seeds for growth after trauma be prematurely planted, ignored, or even inadvertently crushed by us, or will they be nurtured and allowed to flourish by adopting a new perspective toward what has happened? Given this question, the goal for us is to become more mindful, sensitive, and better equipped to begin looking for suitable responses to ourselves and others, including friends, family, and associates who may be going through a post-trauma experience. With proper attention, we can encourage growth *because* of these experiences. Consequently, any knowledge of the process of PTG gained in this chapter and through further reading should prove surprisingly rewarding in our lives. When confronted by such issues in our interpersonal circles, the new perspective we have gained can provide guidance for those of us who wish to go deeper to explore ourselves and become more sensitive in the aftermath of trauma.

While no one would or should wish for a psychological or physical calamity, the paradox we have been discussing is that trauma and serious stress/loss may leave gifts in their wake. Surprisingly, we and others, at times, may fail to open them. One possible reason for this is quite simply we don't know they are there. They may be invisible because there is no expectation of growth from the trauma victim, nor from those who walk alongside them. The hope is that by mere awareness to look, these gifts will indeed be found. But, even when we are fully aware, there is still no guarantee that posttraumatic growth will occur.

As is obvious by now, trying to force growth is immature and not in line with appreciating that some people may not experience significant PTG. But with the support of others, and possibly professional help, hopefully they can at least return to a degree of functioning that parallels, to some extent, their previous life before the trauma, stress, or loss occurred. And so, posttraumatic growth education is about *possibility*: recognizing it and taking advantage of it, while not forcing it. Hopefully, this chapter, along with the following reflection questions and recommended readings listed at the end of the book, will aid in beginning to provide guidance in this very subtle and important process. Certainly, an understanding of growth after trauma is part of fostering a healthier perspective, particularly when times become very tough for us or those we love.

SOME QUESTIONS TO CONSIDER AT THIS POINT . . .

When things get very tough, do you believe you may not be able to remake the world that gave birth to them, but you can remake yourself and the way you view these things in time?

While asking why things have happened is natural after a trauma or loss, do you understand that you will begin to feel better only after you become involved in a new meaning-making process that changes the way you see yourself and the world in which you live?

Do you realize at a deep level that posttraumatic growth isn't simply thinking positive thoughts, but is instead the willingness to face fully the negative aspects of what has happened while simultaneously being open to any new ideas and signs that you are enduring the stress in different ways and even growing/deepening in a previously unimaginable fashion?

After a trauma, loss, or significantly stressful time, are you able to express either in writing or verbally what "pops into your mind" and intrudes in ways that has you ruminating about the event since this process is often a prelude to growth and a healthy transition?

Do you appreciate that trying to make new sense of life after your own worldview and what you believed has been shattered is often an important prelude to new meaning- making and part of both coping and being open to the posttraumatic growth process?

Are you sensitive to, and honoring the presence of, positive emotions after a trauma so their presence isn't clouded over by the also valid negative feelings you are having? (It is important to note that positive emotions such as optimism and feelings of self-efficacy and self-esteem are good predictors of growth. However, equally important is that timing is a key factor as well. The studies suggest that positive emotions come long after the negative event or trauma has ended—*not* in the midst of it.)

Do you encourage yourself to be mindful and stay in the present with what you are experiencing, if it is possible to do so, rather than giving in all the time to the natural temptation to deny, avoid, or minimize?

Can you simultaneously have low expectations and high hopes as to what may come of what you are going through even though it is very unpleasant and discouraging now?

Do you seek out affirming, faithful, and wise relationships that help you in your pursuit of acceptance and arriving at new meaning in your life after experiencing a traumatic event so you can feel free to talk openly and process your losses, fears, angers, and confusion?

If you are among those people described as "persons of faith" or "spiritual persons," are you able to search for support from these aspects of your life and seek guides who can help you do so during such a sensitive period of transition and vulnerability?

Do you realize from both the vantage point of the mindfulness and PTG literature that WHAT has happened (the painful or traumatic event) is important, but HOW you see it—perspective—is especially crucial as well?

FIVE

Uncovering and Facing Inner Roadblocks

Overcoming Resistances to Openness and Change

I have been asked whether there is anything in my life that I regret. I have experiences where I did embarrassing things. I still do plenty of embarrassing things. But there is nothing I regret. When I make a mistake, I repent, accept responsibility, and keep going.

Sheng Yen, *Footprints in the Snow*

No good ever came from putting up walls. What people mistook for safety was in fact captivity. And few things thrived in captivity.

Louise Penny, *A Trick of the Light*

If in the last few years you haven't discarded a major opinion or acquired a new one, check your pulse. You may be dead.

Gelett Burgess

In the following classic dialogue between a wise guide and an aspiring follower, offered by Anthony de Mello, the power of *inner* resistance to openness and change is highlighted:

"How shall I get liberation?"

"Find out who has bound you," said the Master.

> The disciple returned after a week and said, "No one has bound me."
>
> "Then why ask to be liberated?"
>
> That was the moment of Enlightenment for the disciple, who suddenly became free.

If only such instant enlightenment were readily possible! Yet, for most, our journey toward having the healthiest perspective possible is shaped by the way we face and "make friends" with the periodic roadblocks we encounter on our way.

One of the natural arcs for any movement toward openness—and being positioned to have the healthiest perspective—at any given moment is to uncover our resistances to growth and change. Accomplishing this is difficult because defrosting our outlook—especially during emotionally laden moments, when we remain frozen by habits and responses conditioned by society, family, and perhaps now inaccurate, unhelpful beliefs—requires a step-by-step dismantling that is not usually a straightforward process.

When this is done, it can be powerful. Essayist Ralph Waldo Emerson recognized that even the smallest of insights, a slightly clearer perspective or alteration in behavior, ultimately could have amazing results. In his own words,

> Sow a thought and you reap an action;
> Sow an act, and you reap a habit;
> Sow a habit, and you reap a character;
> Sow a character, and you reap a destiny.

A healthy perspective requires openness and leads to actions that may reflect a freshness in our views. Consequently, as best-selling author Roger Housden cautions, "Whatever your circumstances, people will start to give you advice as soon as you disturb the status quo. That advice is likely to be bad. It will be bad because they're seeking not to understand and further your calling but to perceive the world as they know it."

The "people" may be voices that offer counsel or those from our past who left impressions of caution and practicality that subsequently shaped our beliefs. In seeking a healthy perspective, we must uncover and confront them with the question "But is this, should this be, *my* voice *now*?"

I once treated an adult who as a child survived the Holocaust. The understandable neediness and fears of those who raised him drained his early years of carefree spaces and failed to provide the joy and simple security that positive parenting freely offers. The result was his inability to see the nuances of life, a short emotional fuse, and a deep gnawing desire to be emotionally fed *completely, always*. Disagreement was seen as rejection. Close friends were consumed, not cherished. The people around him eventually demonstrated one of the following unsatisfying responses: running away, becoming angry at the demands, "walking on eggs," or avoiding him.

Psychologist and spiritual writer Henri Nouwen, in his book *The Genesee Diary,* describes what can happen to all of us when early experiences mark our own life and prevent us from fostering a healthy perspective on life and love:

> It is important for me to realize how limited, imperfect, and weak my understanding of love has been. Not my theoretical understanding but my understanding as it reveals itself in my emotional responses to concrete situations. My idea of love proves to be exclusive: "You only love me truly if you love others less"; possessive: "if you really love me, I want you to pay special attention to me"; and manipulative: "When you love me, you will do extra things for me." Well, this idea of love easily leads to vanity: "You must see something very special in me"; to jealousy: "Why are you now suddenly so interested in someone else and not in me?" to anger: "I am going to let you know that you have let me down and rejected me."

That is why a healthy circle of friends and an ability to keep our style of interaction with them within reasonable limits is so essential for a rich, balanced, and full life.

A healthy perspective is like poetry. Once again, in the words of Roger Housden in his book on free verse *Ten Poems to Change Your Life,* "Poetry at its best calls forth our deep Being, bids us live by its promptings; it dares us to break free from the safe strategies of the cautious mind; it calls to us, like the wild geese, from an open sky. . . . [A] great poem can open a door in us we may never have known was there." Yet, he also quite rightly adds,

> A new life requires a death of some kind; otherwise it is nothing new, but rather a shuffling of the same deck. What we die

to is an outworn way of being in the world. We experience ourselves differently. We are no longer who we thought we were. But I do not suggest for one moment that it is easy. Nor that there are any guarantees. If you start down a new road, you cannot know where it will take you.

To "break free from safe strategies," we must see perspective in a dramatically different way. It is not the pearl of great price that will give us all that *we* desire now. Instead, a healthy perspective opens us up to see reality more clearly so we can appreciate new possibilities that we would not have imagined if we simply received what we wished. A healthy perspective based on openness doesn't change reality into what we want. Instead, it offers all within the givens of life so that in turn it may become what it might. Alas, "the pearl of great price" often sits right in front of us, unrecognized, untouched, and unengaged.

One of the most precious graces of life is freedom, *inner* freedom. To change, move, *really* grow, we need "space" within ourselves. Habits, worries, emotions, defensiveness, stubbornness, and fear all take up room. Maybe that's why Zen roshis suggests that to find joy and peace, we don't need to *add* something to our lives. Instead, we need to *drop* something so we can see clearly and live more freely. Spiritual figures refer to this as gaining "an unobstructed vision" or "purity of heart." Psychologists are less poetic but just as clear. They simply suggest getting rid of "expensive defenses" that take up all your energy; by uncovering and eliminating old, useless habits and unfounded, erroneous, negative beliefs, the result will be new freedom.

However, while the goal (namely, having space, emptiness, or freedom within) sounds good, it is obviously not easy. Why? It requires us to go completely against the grain of our "common sense" and limited self-awareness. To be free, we must first realize that in many ways we are not!

There are all types of hidden addictions, ingrained habits, and unexamined beliefs that are guiding us automatically and impacting *our* lives negatively. One of the best ways to find out how to engage and expand the healthy aspects is to continually monitor our emotions. Often people feel and then act, but they do not slow down long enough to examine the impulse that started the roller coaster. So pause and ask the questions that will eventually lead to information that frees you.

Self-awareness and sensitivity to what we "fill our psyches with" seems so elusive. I think Thoreau was right when he said, "It is as hard to see oneself as it is to look backward without turning 'round.'" Much of my work is with a "professionally sensitive" population. These "healers" and helpers generally consider themselves in tune with themselves and their environment because of their seminal work and professional roles. Yet those who are truly sensitive are the ones who seek to learn new lessons and "unlearn" old habits each day.

To be aware like that, we must have a questioning habit that is fueled by an appreciation of our emotions. In other words, we need to be able and willing to tune into what our emotions can teach us. When we are angry, sad, thrilled, anxious, fearful, or depressed, we are tempted to think the emotion is being caused by some *external* event in our lives. That is only partly true. The interpretation we attach to the event really plays the major role in eliciting a given emotion.

For example, we might have a friend who asks for book or movie recommendations. Then he calls to criticize the choices. ("The plot is not well developed." "The ending is not believable." "The humor was lagging.") Our first reaction might be, "Well, why do you ask me for suggestions if you are always going to play the critic?"

At our workplace, when someone asks for ideas and then repeatedly rejects them, we may ask a similar question: "Why did you ask if you are only going to reject them (and try to make me feel inferior in the process)?" We may also ask ourselves, "Why is he so critical? Doesn't he know I am going to get tired of it and stop offering suggestions?"

The answer to this is quite simple: "No, he probably doesn't see himself as being critical." Also, in this style of behavior, he may unconsciously feel he will impress you with his own knowledge even though it is off-putting. The reason behind it may be that it is more important for him to feel superior than to have your friendship, for if he valued it, he would be gentler and more sensitive. Fear, which underlies insecurity and neediness, often causes such behavior.

Still, now that we have gone on this "psychoanalytic safari" and analyzed why someone might behave in this irritating fashion, what have we learned that will create more space in our lives? Nothing, really. We may decide either not to suggest anything in the future or just expect he will rarely be happy with our recommendations. But even though we may have made our lives a little more pleasant by the decision, we still haven't opened up any more space in our inner life to change or grow. We haven't yet asked the right type of question. *We haven't questioned far enough.*

We always ask questions about the other persons or events that are precipitating emotions in our lives. This is a natural initial response. In the case just cited, it is normal to ask, "What is the matter with *him*? Why does he behave in such a critical fashion? Doesn't he realize he just pushes potential friends away by being so dissatisfied with suggestions (gifts) offered to him?" Yet, while you may get answers to these inquiries, they are often not the most helpful questions in terms of seeking a healthy perspective on an interaction.

And so, after these outer-directed questions are asked and our emotions of anger or annoyance dissipate a bit, it is time to ask really useful questions, such as, "Why did *I* allow myself to be so upset over someone else's behavior? Or, given my reactions, what can I learn about my own insecurities and agendas that will make me more self-aware, less defensive…more *free*?" Such a change in the focus and extent of our questioning helps us clean our perceptual palate and retrieve the power to alter our future reactions.

If we don't ask these questions or if we stop in the questioning process too soon, we uncover information that might be useful for others but not for ourselves. And the sad part is that it probably won't be useful to them, either. Since their behavior is unconsciously motivated, or is tied to an unexamined belief about themselves and their world, they would naturally deny our interpretation even if we offered it to them on a silver platter. Besides, when we are annoyed by other people's behavior, we are probably the last person able to help them. In such cases, our motivations to help would be less than pure, and our response would more than likely be aimed at paying them back or showing them how they injured us rather benefiting them.

Yet, in irritating and unpleasant situations, we can help ourselves by tilling the psychological and spiritual soil, and planting new self-knowledge that will lead to opportunities for necessary growth and change. How does moodily focusing on the silly behavior of others and our own hurt feelings benefit us? How do we reclaim the power and alter our reactions both interiorly and interpersonally? How we question ourselves—especially when annoyed, hurt, or experiencing a negative emotion—is an important key to self-understanding, changing destructive patterns or reactions, and making space within for new learning opportunities, which are all elements necessary for gaining a healthier perspective.

SWEET DISGUST: WHEN BEING FED UP IS GOOD

In therapy, one of the main reasons people are willing to attempt a program of change is that they are thoroughly fed up with their lives. Such a situation offers a favorable time to risk new attitudes, perceptions, and behaviors in lieu of the status quo. The same holds true for those interested in spiritual wisdom. People come to Hindu swamis, Buddhist rinpoches, Christian mystics, Taoist sages, or Jewish rebbes with the wish to live differently and garner a greater sense of the meaning at the center of their lives. They want their perspective regarding the world transformed, made new.

Whether you call it ingrained habits, unexamined erroneous beliefs, or early life experiences that have led to crippling attitudes in the present, people at this juncture want to both see and experience life differently. They want to *change.*

As the interaction proceeds, the therapist or guru realizes that what is often *really* being asked is this: *Can I change without really changing? Can I alter only those parts of my life that are causing me pain but essentially remain as I am?* This basic resistance to change to a greater sense of openness is natural and to be expected in others and ourselves. Whenever we look at a challenge or problem, we must first and foremost include ourselves in the examination. For many people, the preference is to look outward. But this is insufficient. And so, when the situation gets so bad that they finally want to be off the treadmill of worries, no longer running on the wheel of *suffering,* and are really feeling disgusted with the way they are living, they have a wonderful opportunity to increase self-awareness and vulnerability that enables profound openness to change.

When our attitude and outlook change, our perspective on the whole world around us is altered as well. When a poor man is grateful, his watery soup tastes much better than a wealthy man's fine meal. Furthermore, as we saw in Chapter 3 on gratefulness and happiness, a person who experiences joy within will more often look with a sense of wonder at those around him—as well as at himself.

That is why spending time looking in disgust at the negative patterns in our lives as part of our daily reflection need not be an exercise in masochism. Instead, with the right outlook, it can be a step forward in enlightenment! If this is so, then why don't we do it? Why don't we look at the compulsion, anger, greed, narcissism, and stress in our lives directly and honestly?

Well, I think we fear seeing the truth, and we worry what such insight might demand of us—namely, in our own mind, we may believe we would then need to take action:

- See our *own* role in making our lives a painful web of grasping demands, insecurities, anger, envy, and resentment, and do something about it.
- Become more aware of the time we have lost behaving in a way that has been nonproductive and frozen because we have projected blame outward as an excuse for not doing something inward.
- Face the other's reaction to our new movement toward freedom, love, and peace, and away from competition, defensiveness, and inauthenticity. (The reality is that while other

people say they want us to grow and change, they often feel quite uncomfortable when we do.)

Still, despite our hesitation, being truly fed up with our current ways of perceiving and coping can be the crucial factor in encouraging us toward needed change. Seeing again and again the negative results of our thinking, feeling, and behaving can push us to say, "Enough! I don't want to live this way anymore!" That's a great motivation to begin change. However, staying with it is another story.

In therapy, when people start to get better they are tempted to take a "leap into health" and stop their program of change. In response, the therapist seeks to help them continue to challenge themselves so their overall attitude can be open to new ways of seeing that will open the door to a healthier perspective overall. To make room for such movement, how they and we view life is a determining factor.

PERSONAL INTRIGUE! NOT ARROGANCE OR IGNORANCE

The two greatest enemies of openness and change are *arrogance* and *ignorance*. These two extremes waste more energy than any other defensive maneuver. In fact, if we avoided both of them, growth would happen almost spontaneously and naturally. Zen Buddhists have a great proverb that illustrates this: "Face reality and effortless change will take place."

Arrogance occurs when we export (project) the responsibility for our failures and mistakes. The following words reflect that this process is going on:

- Blaming
- Excusing
- Absolving
- Exploring
- Rationalizing
- Mitigating
- Contextualizing

The more subtle the words and sophisticated our excuses, the more we hide the following central truth from ourselves: *we* have a primary role in removing the blocks to openness and change.

At the other end of the spectrum is *ignorance.* This occurs when we take all of the responsibility for failure in a way that results in our feeling negative about ourselves. Such self-debasement does not lead to insight or personal responsibility. Instead, it ends only in feeling guilty, shameful, or seeing ourselves as failures.

Also, since behavior that we wince at turns into behavior that we wink at, such self-blame eventually burns itself out. So we feel overwhelmed rather than empowered, we are discouraged rather than enlightened, and we avoid further understanding rather than delve deeper for information that will set us free.

Some of the ways we describe this process are

- self-condemnation;
- over-responsibility;
- being hypercritical of self; and
- overly perfectionistic tendencies.

As a positive alternative, seasoned therapists, mentors, and coaches encourage those who seek their guidance to be *intrigued* by their behavior—to be detectives who explore the mystery of the self. Spiritual guides offer the same encouragement. Buddhists, for instance, recommend that people watch themselves objectively—neither condemning nor excusing—so they can see their own grasping tendencies and the evil results such attitudes cause.

Psychological mentors of all sorts often use teasing as a method to show people that they're being overly serious about their mistakes. In response to people condemning themselves, the mentor might say, "I don't think anyone in the city or state has ever made such a creative mistake before!" Breaking up the tension to understand the dynamics, rather than being involved in rumination, is an essential part of intrigue. Furthermore, at the other end of the spectrum, coaches also discourage projecting blame onto others: "If the source of the problem resides fully in the world outside of us, then we will have to change everyone else for it to improve. Quite a job for us!"

When we project blame to others, we also give away the power to change. But if we look at our own role with a sense of intrigue, not self-condemnation, we can increase the power that is within us. This takes practice. Accordingly, I suggest people go through several steps to encourage intrigue:

1. Anytime you have a strong feeling about something, immediately act as if it is someone else experiencing the feeling.
2. Observe any temptation to blame others or condemn yourself.
3. Be a detective who is awed by the subtle temptations to be arrogant/ignorant and get intrigued about the process of uncovering the mystery of the real cause of the problem.

BRING THE RESPONSIBILITIES HOME: NOT WITH VINDICTIVENESS BUT WITH LOVE, AS YOU WOULD A PRODIGAL CHILD

Clarity is the medium for both new freedom and the ability to change. Many people never gain this state because they view the challenges and questions in their life without including the most important factor: *themselves*. Knowing and loving ourselves allows us to be more objective in how we see things. Ignorance, fear, and self-dislike causes our vision to be murky. At times we are so filled with emotion, rationalization, and denial of reality that we are completely blind. No matter. If we understand this, then we can begin to open our psychological and spiritual eyes to see again. Once we do that, we can stand on our own two feet and walk toward our next goal while fully enjoying and learning from the trip itself. Nothing, including pain and failure, is wasted.

So, what will enhance the possibility that we will become increasingly more honest with ourselves as part of gaining a healthier perspective? Whatever would increase the chances for others to accept questions and feedback from us are the same factors that would increase our own willingness to embrace such understandings in ourselves. Included among them are

- style of approach;
- awareness of the positive;
- toughness; and
- willingness to deal with unpleasant specifics.

Style of approach is important if we are to learn the most about ourselves from each event; otherwise learning is blocked out by defensiveness or self-condemnation. Basic to our attitude must be gentleness, love, and crystal-clear honesty. But as our mood changes, so must our approach.

For instance, if we are stressed-out, the approach must be one of gentle intrigue: "Let's see what is happening so we can break things down a bit." A soothing desire to hear ourselves out is an appropriate antidote to anxiety. When we are moody, bored, defeated, or passive, we need to be passionate and encouraging. Maybe we even need to give ourselves a little push to get out of ourselves and reach out to others so we remember to be more grateful for what we have.

Another great way to move toward clarity is to punch holes in the darkness of negative situations. As we have previously appreciated, in line with both cognitive-behavioral therapy (CBT) and positive psychology, this can be done by *increasing our awareness of the positive.* Too often, when we seek greater self-awareness for psychological or spiritual reasons, we raise the volume of our own sensitivity to ourselves. The goal is to bring into consciousness those preconscious games that are hidden from our everyday awareness. To do this, we look at the times we get upset and say to ourselves, "Aha, here is another area where I am holding on!" We also may seek to see in sharper relief those times when we are angry, cowardly, filled with blame for others, pompous, proud, in denial of our own role in making things difficult for ourselves and others, and when we excuse or minimize the negative things we have done and continue to do.

Seeing our faults in the light of day is good. It helps us do something about them. A problem arises, though, when we allow these "clouds" in our lives to gather so we can no longer see our positive gains and achievements. To counter this, we would, as when mentoring others in our family or work circle, recall a time when we were able to change for the better, taking care not to dismiss these successes just because we are failing in our efforts now. When we have raised the volume against solely hearing the defensiveness in our lives, then we can recall when we had the freedom to act and break through our habits, fear, and petty addictions.

Toughness is also important in gaining clarity. All of the techniques in the world designed to enable change and self-awareness won't help us see things more clearly or act on our insights more easily. We must toughen ourselves up so we can face the difficult insights about ourselves in the same way that we embrace the progress.

One spiritual master said to his disciple, "Tell me what you see in me and, in turn, I will tell you what I see in you." His disciple said to him, "You are a good person but a little harsh." In response, the master said, "You are good but your spirit is not tough enough yet." The obvious goal is to build a good and tough spirit in looking at our own foibles, escapes, and excuses.

A willingness to deal with unpleasant specifics in our lives also enhances the possibility that we will be more and more honest with ourselves. Too often our journey in life stays on the "general" level. It can't touch us where we live in daily life. Yet, that is exactly where change must happen. If we wish to be an author but don't write, how will our dream become true? If we say we desire to be more compassionate but treat poorly those who live and work with us, then of what real value is our commitment? Bringing the responsibilities home so we can see clearly our role in the difficulty and then acting to change it means facing what is in front of us. When we do this, the rest of life will follow suit. However, once again, we must follow all of the steps without vindictiveness toward the self. The part of us that needs attention must be seen as a prodigal child welcomed home, to be understood and helped to change, not beaten up—especially by ourselves.

LETTING GO . . . INSTEAD OF GRASPING

We spend so much energy holding onto things and people we feel we must have in order to be happy that we are too exhausted to become involved in a program of change. Change takes energy, openness, and honesty. And, once again, honesty, real honesty with ourselves, requires us to realize that in so many subtle ways we aren't very candid and clear in our self-analysis. As a result, rather than knowing when we are grasping, instead of enjoying life, we stay in the dark, which prevents us from gaining a healthy perspective.

There are many good things: health, wealth, success, friends, feeling physically attractive. To desire and enjoy them is wonderful. Yet, to be dependent on them for our happiness and being anxious all the time about losing them is not good. In our hearts we must be free to appreciate and enjoy all that we have without falling prey to spending much of our time and energy trying to secure them forever.

To hold on tightly many people feel is "only being practical." But in reality it is crazy! If we stopped for a few minutes to reflect on our own and others' experiences, we would see this to be true. There are people who are ill, have little money, are unsuccessful by worldly standards, appear to have few friends, and may not be physically attractive. Yet they are happy.

There are also others—maybe including ourselves at times—who seem to have so much and are not as happy as they could be. Why? Because people who are truly happy have learned to be free to change and enjoy everything that is before them, whereas others have centered on certain things that they feel are the *only* things/persons that will make them happy and are vulnerable to loss. So, unfortunately, when possessions and relationships change, as will surely happen, they then will become unhappy.

Subtle addictions to things, ideas, and people do this to us. While we hold onto what and who we feel will make us happy, we are not loving, free, changing people. Consequently, unhappiness, control, security, and fear become our concern. All our energy goes into this and not into being relaxed and open to change.

Recently, I led a workshop to mentors interested in helping others renew their psychological and spiritual lives by being more open to change. The first message I gave them is that the greatest gift they can offer others is the gentle, interpersonal space for self-examination that can lead to personal change. To do this, they must be willing to see where their own "holding-on energy" is being spent.

To soften them up to seeing those areas, I offered several prediscovery caveats to help reduce the resistance to letting go:

- Anything discovered does not have to be changed immediately.
- No area should be condemned as holding on—just neutrally observed as if it were happening to someone else.

- No area should be defended—no one is criticizing or attacking, just observing where energy is being spent.
- Observations—even disturbing ones—should be embraced as a wonderful treasure trove of information.
- After each period of observation, the areas of concern should be written down so some record is kept of this discovery.

With these provisions in mind, I then offered a principle: *Where there is energy (positive or negative), there is usually grasping and/or fear.* When the smoke of a strong reaction is present, the fire of desire is also usually present, and we need to know what it is. Otherwise, rather than our passions being good energy, they may be products of unexamined attachments.

Once we understand this, we can then look at broad areas of imprisoning and narrow perspective that remain hidden under a veneer of so-called likes, goods, and styles of living. Here are some examples:

Appearance: Everyone likes to look good, but how much energy should we spend toward the effort, and what are our anxieties with respect to weight, hair (dyeing or grooming it, growing a beard), clothes, and so on?

Health: Taking care of oneself is a beautiful way to demonstrate self-respect and value. So, if a person eats too much or too little, takes drugs (including unnecessary medicine), abuses alcohol, doesn't even take a walk for exercise, then there is a problem. The opposite is also true. Some people drive the others in their house to distraction based on their dietary needs. They make exercise a religion, or are so concerned about not gaining weight that they are not attentive or relaxed about themselves but preoccupied and practically anorexic.

Image: Wanting to know how we are coming across is fine. However, once again, if there are inordinate concerns about being appreciated, liked, seen as helpful, intelligent, or attended to, then there is a problem.

Control: It is good to feel one has the freedom to some control over one's destiny and to have a positive impact on others. Yet, as in the other sample areas cited, this also can be an area where we wish too much control. The irony is we often have the opposite impact when too much energy is expended here. By being so concerned about being in charge of our own lives, we fail to take enough risks that in the end would give us more security. Those who invested all their money in bonds and government securities in the 1960s–1990s lost retirement earning power compared with those who put some or all of their money into the stocks of established companies. Paradoxically, parents who are too controlling with their children, and employers who are too overbearing with their employees, usually breed rebellion in the very people they wish to influence.

So, in varied aspects of our lives, we need to ask a simple question: *When do I get upset or feel the happiest?* Our answer will lead to wonderful information about our values and preferences. It will also guide us to those places where we have become frozen, excluding other possibilities for ourselves and others. Once again, feeling joy is wonderful, and being upset on occasion is natural. The problem is not with the emotion or experience but in knowing why we really feel this way. By questioning ourselves further, there is so much helpful information for us to mine that will lead us to gaining a healthier perspective. To reinforce this, we should also seek to emulate those people we admire for their openness and psychological health.

LOOKING MORE CLOSELY: SHARPENING A HEALTHY PERSPECTIVE THROUGH DAILY "SELF-DEBRIEFINGS"

Annie Dillard, in her book *The Writing Life,* notes, "In working-class France, when an apprentice got hurt or when he got tired, experienced workers said, 'It is the trade entering his body.'" Similarly, when the daily pressures of our lives seem to tip the scale, we too become tired and frustrated; it is a rich, meaningful, and compassionate life entering our body.

A life of caring is never easy and sometimes pushes us into irritation. After a day especially filled with aggravations and ridiculous requests, a pastor sat down to dinner with his hair all askew, said a prayer of thanks, turned to his dinner guest, and said with a sigh, "I get the feeling that early this morning someone put a sign on the door that read: If you're nuts, knock here!"

Sometimes things get much worse than this, though. As we listen to stories of terrible things that happen to a family member or coworker, we catch some of their futility, fear, vulnerability, and hopelessness rather than experiencing mere frustration or concern. We learn that no matter how professionally prepared we are, we are not immune to the psychological and spiritual dangers that arise in living a full life of involvement with others. I remember learning this the hard way myself.

In 1994 I did a psychological debriefing of some of the relief workers evacuated from Rwanda's bloody civil war. I interviewed each person and gave them an opportunity to tell their stories. As they related the horrors they had experienced, they seemed to be grateful for an opportunity to vent. They recounted the details again and again, relating their feelings as well as descriptions of the events that triggered them. Their sense of futility, their feelings of guilt, their sense of alienation, and their experiences with emotional outbursts, all came to the fore.

In addition to listening, I gave them handouts on what to possibly expect down the road (problems sleeping, difficulties trusting and relating to others, flashbacks, and the like). As I moved through the process of debriefing and providing information so they could have a frame of reference for understanding their experiences, I thought to myself, "This is going pretty well." Then, something happened that shifted my whole experience.

In the course of one of the final interviews, one of the relief workers related stories of how certain members of the Hutu tribe raped and dismembered their Tutsi foes. Soon, I noticed I was holding onto my chair for dear life. I was doing what some young people call "white knuckling it."

After the session, I did what I usually do after an intense encounter—a psychospiritual, countertransferential review. (If time doesn't permit then, I do it at the end of the day—every day.) In doing this, I get in touch with my feelings by asking myself, "What made me sad? Overwhelmed me? Sexually aroused me? Made me extremely happy or even confused me?" Being brutally honest with myself, I try to put my finger on the pulse of my emotions.

The first thing that struck me about this particular session was the tight grip I had on the chair as the session with the relief worker progressed. "What was I feeling when I did this? Why did I do this?"

It didn't take me long to realize that their terrible stories had broken through my defenses and temporarily destroyed my normal sense of distance and detachment. I was holding onto the chair because, quite simply, I was frightened to death that if I didn't, I would be pulled into the vortex of darkness myself.

That recognition alone helped lessen the pain and my fearful uneasiness. I then proceeded with a combination of a countertransferential review and theological reflection. These are tools used by therapists and ministers to prevent the slide into unnecessary darkness and to learn—and thus benefit—from the events of the day.

For therapists and counselors, a countertransferential review helps them get in touch with the feelings they have had in their treatment sessions. They seek to discover whether their intense encounters with the persons they serve triggered distorted thoughts and beliefs. By looking at their own reactions, they not only learn things about themselves but also appreciate the people and situations they encounter in new ways.

For ministers, a theological reflection is a spiritual review of the day. In the process, they too stop at the end of the day to take stock of their lives. This, like the countertransferential review, helps them to catch the slide into unnecessary darkness and learn from difficult or intense events.

The process of a *structured reflection*, which could be modified according to individual needs, includes the following steps:

- Choose events during the day that stand out.
- Enter into the event and describe what happened (the objective) and how we felt (the subjective).
- See what we can learn from the event about ourselves and our vulnerabilities, needs, addictions, fears, anxieties, worries, and desires. Avoid the temptation to become discouraged or to blame others (projection) or ourselves (self-condemnation).
- Reflect on this learning in light of what we believe (our philosophy, psychology, ethics, and/or spirituality).

- Decide how this learning should change us personally, interpersonally, and professionally.
- Alter the way we behave in light of these new insights.

In the Buddhist tradition, Zen roshis teach that feelings, past hurts, shame, questions, and needs will surface during meditation. These can teach us, if we are willing to pay attention to and refrain from judging, blaming, indulging in, or rejecting our feelings. We must be open to learn from these experiences. In his informative work *A Path with Heart,* Jack Kornfield points out, "Spiritual transformation is a profound process that doesn't happen by accident. We need a repeated discipline, a genuine training, in order to let go of our old habits of mind and to find and sustain a new way of seeing. To mature on the spiritual path we need to commit ourselves in a systematic way."

We all can benefit from these processes—be it countertransferential review, philosophical/theological reflection, or Buddhist meditation. People who wish to live truly aware lives need to take time out during the day or at day's end to quietly sit with their feelings and cognitions in an objective, nonjudgmental way. The more we do this on a regular basis, the more we can avoid unnecessary darkness while we live through the unpleasant events of life in a way that provides direction and learning.

We can enhance debriefing ourselves by sharing this process with someone we trust to accompany us on the psychological and spiritual journey. When we get feedback from those we trust, we cut down on the distortion and discouragement that arises when we seek to be truly honest and loving with ourselves. The importance of having the patience and determination to go deeper in our lives sometimes can't be seen until someone else, much wiser than we are, helps nudge us along in the self-discovery process. A sensitive guide who was aware of the important role balance plays in exploring our inner life once told me this story, which nicely illustrates my point:

> As I reflected on a call I felt to metaphorically "Put out into the deep water and lower my nets for a catch," a childhood memory came to mind. My aunt would advise me on how to draw a cup from a fresh pail of milk. The cream and froth would be gathering to the top, and if you put your mug in straight, it either filled with froth (no substance, shallow) or with all the cream (too rich for your system).
>
> Instead she showed me how to bend over and blow gently on the top, about three gentle blows. The froth and cream would glide over to the sides and I could then put my mug in deep down and draw up milk and angle my cup in such a way to gather just a little cream as well.

Beautiful! But we have to be willing to patiently, gently, blow the froth and to reach into the depth and draw up such a full, balanced catch.

A "full, balanced catch" involves discovering

- what we were *feeling* (affect) at different points in the day;
- what we were *thinking* that caused us to feel that way; and

- what we were *believing* that made us think or come up with the conclusions.

Not to review and learn from our day is foolish. Moreover, if we don't constantly spend time asking ourselves about why we feel, think, and believe what we do, we will ruin the chance to live a freer, more satisfying life. When we employ ways to enhance openness to change and increase clarity, we foster both a healthier perspective and a way of greeting each day that results in our discovering more about ourselves and those around us (see Box 10).

Box 10 In Pursuit of Clarity: Careful Self-Questioning

The world fears a new experience more than it fears anything. Because a new experience displaces so many old experiences.
D.H. LAWRENCE

Simple exploration of events, feelings, and cognitions (ways of thinking, perceiving, and understanding) can provide a wonderful resource for reflection, adjusting dysfunctional thinking, changing our perspective to a healthier one, and ultimately producing important changes in both our attitude and behavior. Here are some sample questions that are driven by principles from critical thinking, cognitive-behavioral and schema therapy, as well the classic spiritual discernment literature.

Box 10 (Continued)

When I fail, do I

- Ask myself what I feel most badly about for not succeeding?
- Catch myself when I am tempted to see everything as a failure instead of this one event?
- Give myself the alonetime necessary to be upset, understand, and move on?
- See how my own ego is preventing me from being open to all the agendas and learning possible?
- Appreciate what I can learn about myself that would not have been possible had I succeeded?
- Learn what contributed to this failure both in myself and in the situation surrounding it?
- Appreciate how to avoid or minimize failures like this in the future without feeling I must totally withdraw from the scene as a way of dealing with the lack of success in this instance?
- See the role of unrealistic expectations and how my own thinking may have contributed to those expectations?
- See how failure and the pacing of efforts in my life are possibly related because I was moving too fast, slow, or precipitously?
- Acknowledge personal and professional limitations in my life that can be improved?
- Miss early warning signs that if addressed could have averted this result?

- See this as an impetus to initiate new interpersonal approaches to the challenge in question?
- Recognize that failure is part and parcel of involvement and that the more I am involved, statistically, the more I will fail?

Do I emulate cognitive behavioral and schema therapists as well as critical thinkers and spiritual guides by seeking the wisdom, intellectual power, and healthier perspective that can result from more carefully

- Examining comfortable, but unsatisfying patterns with an eye to practicing a step-by-step approach to undo and replace them?
- Recognizing my own gifts, growing edges, agendas, negative emotions, attitudes, motivations, beliefs, and ways of thinking, perceiving, and understanding when a feeling or reaction arises?
- Seeing "the grays" of life rather than simply shunning ambiguities and seeking only "right" or "wrong" answers to life's questions?
- Entertaining both the possible and probable as I reflect on a challenge, problem, or question?
- Appreciating (and then enjoying more fully) the positive elements already present in my interpersonal circle?
- Uncovering when I overpredict worrisome events and challenging them so even little potentially beautiful encounters in life aren't missed?

(*continued*)

Box 10 (Continued)

- Appreciating those times when I tend to exaggerate, catastrophize, minimize, "awfulize," or can't see the humor or nuance in events or interpersonal encounters?
- Dealing with disagreement, rejection, or change?
- Searching for what I can understand and letting go when I encounter personal, emotional, hot-button issues?
- Picking up defeating "self-talk," such as minimizing or disqualifying the positive: "If I feel it, it must be true," "If I don't succeed at something then I am a total failure," and so on?
- Balancing the way I am looking at an event by exploring alternative possibilities/interpretations?
- Recognizing an inclination to see negative and self-defeating behaviors as being a "natural" part of one's life rather than a schema/belief to be uncovered, challenged, and replaced with a healthier perspective/life pattern?

Do I seek further clarity in examining something during my daily debriefing by discovering the following:

- What emotions are elicited by this particular topic, event, or area, and what is the thinking behind them?
- What mature and immature agendas do/did I have in this interaction?
- On what am I basing my conclusions/interpretations regarding this, and what might be some other possible

ones that I might see now that I have stepped back from the interaction/event?

- What makes this challenge a possibly more difficult or emotional one for me?
- What might be some other ways to look at this that I haven't yet considered?
- Are there additional details or input I could obtain that might help me broaden or deepen my understanding?
- Why might I resist changing my opinion on this? What consequences or vulnerabilities are in play here?
- What was unexpected and surprising in what I am now examining?
- What is the first thing that comes to mind when I think of this topic/event/person, and what can this reaction teach me about *myself*?
- Am I giving enough time for reflection and consideration of the issues at hand?
- Am I picking up the "voices" of self/other blame, discouragement, and unhelpful labeling of people and events so my response to them prevents critical thinking?
- What factors do parental/family/corporate/religious/other values and notable past events in my life play in preventing me from thinking more openly about this issue?
- What would it take for me to replace possible hypersensitivity with a sense of intrigue about these events or occurrences?

(*continued*)

Box 10 (Continued)

- How can I use this particular issue to practice resilience building and strengthen a healthier perspective by (1) leaning back emotionally from the event; (2) reappraising it; and (3) renewing myself through gaining new wisdom through humility and new learning?
- How does this opportunity increase my sense of intrigue about where I am spending my energy and learning what the emotional centers of gravity are in my life?
- How can I develop new abilities in asking myself questions, developing logic and abstract reasoning, clarifying my values, and collecting as much information as possible in ways that increase my self-knowledge and enjoyment of all of life (both what is perceived as bad as well as good)?
- How do I innovatively approach tracking dysfunctional styles, enhancing life-giving activities and approaches, and becoming fascinated with learning more ways to loosen the grasp of ongoing unproductive habits?
- How do I entertain views that possibly oppose my own but which may balance or enrich my understanding?
- How do I understand my unfamiliar and familiar actions?
- Where does immediate self-interest blind me to new information that may lead to a broader, healthier perspective for me in the long run?

If we avoid looking at ourselves, we don't get a chance to uncover the hidden programming that may be driving us in directions we need not go. On the other hand, by taking the time to examine ourselves during the day and at day's end, we get a chance to cut the psychological strings being held by the "hidden puppeteer" (our unconscious or hidden erroneous beliefs) and live our lives in a clearer, more intentional way. Obviously, this is essential if we are to live peaceful, full, and compassionate lives and are to have healthy perspectives.

BRINGING ROLE MODELS CLOSER SO THEY CAN HELP US

There is a tendency to keep potential role models at a distance. The media colludes in this regard. It first elevates people who are very different from us. Then investigative reporters dig up every little bit of dirt they can to show us that the idols they provided for us have clay feet. This provides a seesaw effect on our psyche and can be discouraging. We get a message that is very disheartening: namely, that real wisdom figures and truly good persons are rare—if they exist at all!

This message is pure nonsense! Moreover, it is destructive to the natural and needed movement in society to both seek and be mentors. All of us should try to be role models for others—not by being fake or putting on a good face in a particular role, but by being all that we can be. Each day (it is too discouraging if we try to do this for longer periods of time), we need to accept the challenge to be the best we can be at home, in the office—and even in the grocery store.

Again, by this, I don't mean we should practice "chronic niceness" and put on a plastic smile. Nor do I mean we should seek to be like someone famous or familiar who has a lifestyle or personality that is nothing like ours. What is essential is that we seek to be a healthy role model, while also seeking a personal standard bearer for ourselves. Our role model should be the kind of person we believe we would look like if we dropped some of our defenses and let our personality flourish.

In psychotherapy, patients are able to change partly because the therapist functions at some level as a role model. The patients say to themselves, "I trust that this person, while not perfect, is living in truth, with greater flexibility, and an openness to greater possibility than I am now. I can follow her lead. I can borrow her strength and try, step by step, to risk change, to explore new possibilities and ways of viewing myself and the world (a healthy perspective)."

In spiritual guidance, the role of a sage also is essential. In Buddhism and Hinduism it is devotion to a *guru* (literally meaning "one who removes darkness") and a deep desire to join one's will with that of this spiritual master. In Christianity, it may be Christ, who in the Gospels tells Christians that he chose not to cling to his divinity so that people could see their own humanity and possibility in him.

In daily life, there are lessons and opportunities like this for all of us as well. In business, there may be a person whom we admire. In our families, an older sibling or cousin may have a similar personality style to our own but be more personally integrated. Or, in a well-developed saga or biography we have read, we may see possibilities in others that we wish to emulate.

For years I felt a need to be more gentle as a way of softening my passion. In Shirley du Boulay's biography of Bede Griffiths, *Beyond the Darkness,* I saw his desire for gentleness was somewhat like mine. I saw that his nature needed toning as mine did and still does. But du Boulay's words about Griffiths gave me hope when I first read them and they continue to do so:

> It is clear that as a young man Alan was not easy to live with; that the saintly man he was to become was the result of his determination, the fruit of a life of . . . meditation, rather than the path of a man born with a naturally easy temperament. The search for holiness, the journey on which he was already embarking, is a hard road. If he sometimes overrode the needs of his companions, it was the blindness brought on by the intensity of his own struggle and he certainly paid for it in the remorse that later swept over him. Much later Hugh [Bede's old friend] summed up the way Alan had been and the man he became in a single phrase: "He is much more now a pervasive light than a consuming flame."

One of the big elements of change, then, is to seek out role models whom we can emulate rather than keep at a distance. To increase the chance that this will happen, we need to find ones that are right for us at this point in our lives.

Role models vary from person to person. One person may seek someone who is inspirational. For another, the primary valued trait is the ability to be a clear thinker, or to have a calm demeanor. However, when we think of role models and our emulating them with respect to "inner freedom," "growth," "change," and "a healthy perspective," certain talents or gifts are present in some form in all truly healthy role models, no matter what their personality style or background is. And so, it is important to identify those talents or gifts. Not only does it help in the choice of a person to emulate, but this is essential to know when we try to develop our own inner freedom. In this way, we are able to actively welcome growth and change, rather than resist it.

Some of the key talents of a role model who embodies inner freedom and a healthy perspective include the following:

- Is able to let go
- Welcomes new lessons
- Maintains a countercultural attitude that is not self-righteous
- Holds a sense of intrigue with one's own emotional flashing lights
- Feels disgust with *samsara* (the endless wheel of suffering that comes from grasping and attachments) and bad habits

- Cultivates curiosity, not judgment
- Values experience
- Recognizes danger of preferences which prevent experiencing new gifts in life
- Is mindful; awake to the present
- Appreciates quiet meditation
- Offers generosity and is alive
- Learns, reflects, and applies wisdom in daily life
- Rests lightly in life
- Knows the difference between "freedom to be" versus "freedom to choose"

To get a sense of these people, who have such a healthy sense of perspective that freedom is enhanced in them as well as those who encounter them and are open, let us close with questions that are commonly asked of such mentors of mindfulness and clarity. In this case, the sample responses that follow represent composites of the type of responses offered by masters from different spiritual traditions.

SAMPLE QUESTIONS TO CONSIDER AT THIS POINT . . .

What is the psychological essence of inner freedom?

Don't prejudge. Picasso used to lament that it was a shame we couldn't pluck out our brain and use just our eyes. Too often, past experience fastens a biased perception onto what we encounter. This prevents us from seeing things simply as they are.

Instead, we see things as we wish them to be, as we fear they might be, or as we feel they should be. Wishes, fears, and shoulds cloud our eyes and prevent clarity.

Are there signs that I'm not open to the help I've sought from others?

The following are classic signs that we are resisting help from others to grow or change:

- Frequently arguing or taking issue with suggestions being offered
- Holding back on sharing information because of shame or lack of trust
- Making excuses for not doing the agreed-upon tasks between sessions/meetings with your growth/change consultant/mentor
- Complaining that real progress is too difficult for you to accomplish
- Blaming others for your lack of advancement
- Focusing on the differences between you and your mentor as a way of excusing your lack of compliance with suggestions offered for consideration
- Monopolizing time together to the extent that the other person can't get in a word
- Being late or missing helpful encounters with others
- Not taking responsibility for bringing information to a meeting, but expecting that the consultant will provide the agenda
- Repeating extended silent periods

Are there ever times when disagreement with someone guiding me is not resistance to change but a healthy difference?

Yes, when you have different philosophies with respect to life goals. This most frequently happens in work situations when you are being given feedback by someone who is, in the organizational chart, responsible for mentoring you. (For instance, in one man's end-of-year evaluation, his supervisor said, "You are so talented I'm surprised you are not more ambitious." After reflecting on this feedback, the man replied to his boss, "Oh, I think I'm very, very ambitious. However, I think we may be ambitious for different things." When he explained to his supervisor what he meant by this, both recognized true value differences rather than the worker's resistance to risking and expending energy to move ahead.)

What are some of the ways I can reduce my resistance to the change and growth I seek when I work with someone (a coach, supervisor, mentor, therapist, spiritual guide)?

If you are willing to consult someone to help you change and grow, you have already overcome the first block that most people never get beyond: namely, the simple admission that you need assistance. You can't do it alone. Once you've taken that step, you can take advantage of your consultant by following some simple, but often not easy, guidelines:

- Be honest.
- Avoid second-guessing or preparing answers while your consultant is speaking. Instead, listen carefully.

- Clarify, as much as possible, what your goals are in seeking this relationship; ensure you both are in agreement regarding the objectives.
- Recognize that although the principles of change, growth, and achieving greater freedom are usually surprisingly simple, they take work.

Is there a style of thinking I should seek to incorporate that encourages growth, change, and the search for a healthier perspective?

Yes. If you see yourself as an adventurer, or part of a group of psychological and spiritual pioneers, as people in the forefront of creative business, like inventors Thomas Edison and Buckminster Fuller were, you will become excited about the very process of change. Even failures will teach and intrigue you. The important attitude that encourages this type of thinking is this: I will enjoy the process or journey toward greater freedom, change, and enlightenment and not just focus on the end result.

What about the other side of the coin? What tip-offs do I have that my thinking is resisting change by being defeatist, inappropriate, or negative, and how can I short-circuit self-defeating thinking?

Real change becomes difficult when we are ambushed by negative beliefs and unhelpful attitudes. All real growth, and a healthy perspective, requires that we surface and answer the messages that have held us back—maybe even for years!

Catch yourself making broad, negative statements and answer them:

Answer the thought "I'm a failure" with "I didn't succeed this time. What can I learn from what happened?"

Respond to "I guess I am just not meant to change or grow" with "What happened today that I found discouraging?" "Why am I so discouraged?" and "Did I set my goals in a way that they were meant to deflate rather than to challenge me?"

Replace "Changing is impossible! It's just too hard" with "Change is hard, but it is a process. Progress will occur with some work and keeping each step manageable."

And instead of "My life is hopeless; I need to win 'a psychological lottery,'" remember that "When things don't go our way, it may feel hopeless, but when we break things down and take it step-by-step, there's reason for hope."

People say you can also use humor to dispute irrational thinking that's holding you back. I'm a fairly serious person, so what can I do to tease myself so I can see how ridiculous my beliefs or reactions are?

One way is to *exaggerate* something to the point of the absurd. You can tell yourself the following when you fail: "It is the worst thing that has ever happened in the world. No one in the world has ever made a mistake like this!"

The Calm within the Storm: An Epilogue

The greatest good you can do for another is not just share your riches but to reveal to him his own.

Benjamin Disraeli

When learned optimism is coupled with a renewed commitment to the [common good], our epidemic of depression and meaninglessness may end.

Martin Seligman, *Authentic Happiness*

When the tide rises, the boats also rise.

Chinese Proverb

When we experience the freedom and clarity that accompanies having a healthy perspective, it usually is a breath of fresh air for others. In the words of Jack Kornfield in his delightful and thought-provoking book *After the Ecstasy, the Laundry*, "The understanding of emptiness [what I would call having a healthy perspective] is contagious: It appears we can catch it from one another. We know that when a sad or angry person enters a room, we too often enter into sadness or anger. It shouldn't surprise us, then, that the presence of a teacher who is empty, open, awake can have a powerful effect on another person, especially if that person is ripe."

When we have space within ourselves that results from the process of seeking a healthy perspective, it gives others the room to experience themselves in different ways, to try out new behaviors, and entertain ideas that may be foreign to them until this point. They sense a calm hospitality that says to them that

- life need not be this way;
- the way you think now, even if you have experienced trauma, need not always be the final word or the whole story; and
- each day there is a new story if you are ready to listen to yourself without prejudgment.

People are often so driven and compulsive, anxious or stressful, sad or doubtful. Life is stormy for them. With a perspective that calls us to be faithful to the truth and not concerned about success, we can meet such turmoil in others with a gentle sense of calmness. With no need for people to get somewhere we need them to go, they are able to pace themselves as they wish. There is no pressure, only a place to be, explore, and maybe see life more clearly, in different ways, with less desire and demand, and with more gratitude and a greater sense of *intrigue*. It is a beautiful invitation of hospitality offered to others—one that we may also have already accepted, or are currently accepting, from someone we respect.

A psychiatrist's wife once questioned him about the reason he remained loyal to his mentor, the Zen master Shunryu Suzuki. She wondered why he was so faithful to the guidance he was receiving. He responded by saying, "Where he is, is where

I want to be, in that place of sanity." The "place" he speaks about is where all of us wish to be—not only for ourselves, but also for others: so we can invite them into this precious space, which is tantamount to being the calm within the storm. This is a great gift because it is not the natural reaction of many people. As Henri Nouwen notes, "Compassion is hard because it requires the inner disposition to go with others to the place where they are weak, vulnerable, lonely, and broken. But this is not our spontaneous response to suffering. What we desire most is to move away from suffering by fleeing from it or finding a quick cure for it."

And so, reaching out without being pulled down involves practicing an ability to psychologically "lean back" rather than step out of the encounter entirely. The opposite of detachment from emotionally laden situations is *not* compassion—it is seduction. In such instances, we are drawn in by the unrealistic demands of others and our own archaic superego (rigid conscience that leads to guilty feelings) rather than "simply" asking ourselves, "What can we realistically do?" and then being faithful in doing it. The perception many have of the helping process is often fraught with unrealistic expectations that have a negative impact not only on the helping situation but also on the helper's mood. Focusing on faithfulness rather than success and having a greater awareness of our own motivations/perspectives for and on helping is key to reaching out to our family, friends, and coworkers in the most beneficial way possible—which is not always easy for people to remember to do in an emotional situation.

Years ago I met a fascinating negative character. She wasn't a depressive, but, as they say today—she certainly was a carrier! She was a true silver lining looking for a cloud. However, if you were careful not to be pulled into meeting her demands or wanting to force her to enjoy life, you could see she had many wonderful traits.

By not personalizing her intermittent negative comments, and through the use of humor, I was able to actually enjoy her inner beauty. I didn't try to show her how much she was missing by not being more grateful and energetic. Her family repeatedly attempted this and ended up only being frustrated and quietly resentful of her. Instead, I simply stood back a little and let her be herself. Then, I would let her know I realized the trouble she was having. She responded to this by being grateful to me for appreciating her plight.

Because I didn't try to "fix" her, we enjoyed one another as much as we could. By having a little distance from her constant negative comments and by decreasing the expectations I might normally have for someone truly interested in change, I did not get pulled into her negative cloud as often or as easily. When I did—because she was a master at making people feel guilty—I just woke myself up to the fact that I wasn't on my guard, laughed at myself, and tried again. Actually, by making it into a game like that, it even turned out to be fun.

Later I helped her adult children to enjoy her more as well. I had to use a rather strange technique so they, too, could see it as a game. I told them that when they visited her or chatted with her on the phone, they had to imagine that (a) they were speaking to someone they didn't know (to create distance) and (b) she had been committed for long-term mental treatment and was not in touch with reality at all. (In this way, they would have no expectations that their mother was going to be able to comfort or respond positively to them, as much as they would have loved such a response.) With constant practice, the negative bonds were broken and most of the time they were able to be present to their mother in a way that didn't hurt them yet allowed their mother to get the attention she needed. By pruning their expectations, their availability was richer, less destructive, and more rewarding to all involved. They also were more open to receiving from others what they couldn't and weren't receiving from their mother, and this was another plus.

Persons in the helping professions also at times lose distance and are temporarily swept away by the expectations, needs, and painful experiences of others. More than most people, they are confronted with negativity and sadness. Yet they are educated to pick up these emotional signs as early as possible so they are not unnecessarily dragged down. Every one of us can learn much from what such helpers do to avoid losing perspective and on how they regain it after temporarily losing their way in reaching out to others. The distance they value can help us deal with the pain of others in our own family, at work, and in our own circle of friends.

There is much benefit to remembering the Russian proverb "When you live next to the cemetery, you can't cry for everyone who dies." Yet the reality is that most of us, whether we are professional helpers or not, if we are caring, have a tendency to personalize the negativity and suffering of others. We tend to absorb the sadness, anxiety, and helplessness of those around us. Sometimes we even feel this is expected of us. Moreover, sometimes we sense that if we don't cry when our children fail, if we don't get stressed out by our spouse's temporary unhappiness, if we don't feel paralyzed by the injustices in society, then we think others—or perhaps even ourselves—will believe we just don't care.

All caring people must come to grips with the danger of being negatively infected by those they support. Otherwise, they will not only become too stressed out to continue, but they will also face burnout and negativity in their interactions with the very persons for whom they are caring. Knowing the information that professional helpers use to prevent this is especially helpful. To set the stage, there are three basic principles to remember to keep a healthy perspective and truly be a calm, healing presence when surrounded by the turmoil of others:

1. *Everyone becomes overwhelmed once in a while.* That's natural. However, when we have a pattern of being pulled down, we need to change our perspective with respect to how we relate to others, or it will become habitual.
2. *Caring means being willing to keep enough distance* from those we love or are concerned with so we are able to avoid drowning

with them in their problems. This takes a willingness to forgo the "luxury of being upset" while a person is sharing his or her problem.

3. *Knowing the signals of overinvolvement helps avoid burnout.* Recognizing our "red flags of emotion" before things get out of control is essential. Otherwise, we step over an emotional cliff, arguing or crying with someone when a clear head is really what is needed. This would be a wonderful gift to offer those we are trying to support.

EVERYONE BECOMES OVERWHELMED ONCE IN A WHILE

Knowing we make mistakes at times relieves us of the temptation to erect new protective boundaries and, in the process, possibly make the situation worse. When people know they should keep a distance (so they are not pulled into another's pain) but still get drawn in, they sometimes complicate matters by how they react. They either pick on themselves for getting caught into a web of anger and stress, or they blame the other person for upsetting them. For example, a parent allows herself to be pulled into an argument with a teenage daughter, then later blames both herself and her child for losing her temper. As she ruminates about it for the rest of the day, she swings between guilt and self-recrimination on the one hand, and resentment of her daughter on the other.

The reality is that no matter how much experience we have even as professional helpers, we all get drawn in once in a while. The same can be said to a greater degree in the case of those who have not received specialized training in helping others. The important thing is to try to learn from it each time it happens:

1. *Recognize the emotional signals*—anger, sadness, fear, anxiety, feeling overwhelmed, pity—and lean back. For example, be quiet or excuse yourself for a moment, even leave the room to get some distance.
2. *Don't condemn yourself or the other person* who is probably also experiencing similar negative emotions about the encounter. Instead be curious about your reactions so you can learn from them and gain power over how you react in the future.
3. *Try to figure out what the early signals* are of being drawn in so you can see how you may improve your interactions in the future.

CARING MEANS BEING WILLING TO KEEP ENOUGH DISTANCE

Being upset is easy. Practically all of us can get teary-eyed at certain times when watching a sad movie. However, having the discipline to keep enough distance from the emotions of the moment is a real gift to those who turn to us for help and support. Once while I was chatting with a visitor, a coworker stepped into my office. She told us a story about a terrible tragedy in her life. While my visitor got very upset, I tried to step back, listen to her, figure out how I could stand with her, and give her some clear feedback.

After she left, my visitor asked how I could hear the story and not get upset. I told him that she really saw his caring in the fact that he felt for her. But I saw my role differently as trying to help, much as a surgeon would in an operation. Each of us—in a different way—supported her.

"But weren't you upset?" he persisted.

"Yes, I was. But when I started to get upset, I told myself to put my feelings on hold until this evening when I could sit and be with them." By doing this, I felt I could not only be helpful to her but I could reflect later on the feelings I had. Then, at a better time and in a safer place, *I could let them move away from me so I didn't push them down or get caught in them in the future.* (This last process is also important to keeping a healthy perspective and emotionally free space within us to avoid being psychologically contaminated to the extent that we temporarily lose psychological equilibrium and, in turn, diminish our ability to be present and help in some way—even if "only" as an empathic listener, which is a great, often underrated gift in itself.)

KNOWING THE SIGNALS OF OVERINVOLVEMENT HELPS AVOID BURNOUT

The sooner we experience and note our emotional reactions, the greater the possibility we won't be drawn in or pulled down by them. Too often we don't do this because we think the external event is what is causing the reaction. This leads to foolish thinking that often causes us problems and doesn't allow us to uncover new information that might help. If someone cuts us off on the highway, he or she is demonstrating inappropriate and dangerous behavior. But how much more foolish are we when we respond with anger and raised blood pressure? Yet people do this all the time and feel it is a natural reaction. Well, it may be common—but it's also unhelpful and unproductive.

The more we use our reactions to learn how we are giving away power, the more vital we will remain and continue to become. The ultimate goal in picking up our red flags of emotion is to change our spontaneous negative reactions into spontaneous neutral—or even positive—ones. When we do this, we will save energy, be in a more receptive place to learn about ourselves, and live a life in which both positive and negative events can be greeted as teachable moments.

No one likes moments of stress and anxiety. Nor do we enjoy emotions such as anger, resentment, or sadness. The general tendency is to react to them by withdrawing, blaming, being overly cautious, or becoming discouraged. However, this doesn't mean that we shouldn't be alert and address them. In the process of seeking a healthier perspective—especially during times when we are extending ourselves to others—we need to allow our emotions to be signals of potential teachable moments. This can be better done by

- seeing the signals of distress we are experiencing;
- distancing ourselves by observing ourselves and the event as if it were happening to someone else;
- avoiding blame of self or others; and
- asking how and what we learn about ourselves from these experiences.

Incorporating a learning paradigm for distressful moments is a proven method therapists use with themselves and, through modeling during a session (by reflecting rather than immediately reacting), also teach their clients. It is an approach that mentors, coaches, and spiritual guides also employ with those who turn to them for help in recognizing their attachments (for example, their image, being liked, or grasping rather than enjoying certain material things in life). In this way, they can see the cost of this silent slavery and can continue on the road to true freedom and a life of less stress and suffering. Obviously, it would benefit us to do the same.

An accepting, clear presence to others is both simple and powerful, but experience teaches us that change is by no means easy. We gain in so many ways, even when our efforts seem to fail, because in being available to others with the right perspective we

- listen to, and become part of, other people's often intense, and sometimes amazing, narratives;
- have a chance to make a difference;
- experience new intimacy;
- have an opportunity to observe the courage to change and, in the process, see where we might need to be bold in our own lives as well;
- become "detectives" who walk with others seeking clues to how a healthier perspective in their lives can be found;
- appreciate the need for "alonetime" to balance our interpersonal times—especially ones with demanding people in our network;
- learn to develop new problem-solving skills and creativity as we are confronted by a myriad of people with a portfolio of challenges; and
- deal with failure better since statistically, the more we are involved with people under stress, the more we run the risk of not succeeding as we or they wish.

A FINAL COMMENT

A program on developing, maintaining, and regaining a healthy perspective (when we lose it, as certainly we shall at different points during the day and in life) should be one with differing routes to experience greater freshness in how we encounter life as it unfolds. After periods of mindfulness and reflection on the lessons of cognitive behavioral therapy, positive psychology, narrative therapy, the psychology of gratitude and happiness, posttraumatic growth, ways to debrief ourselves, and even understanding and utilizing what we learn from *our own* resistance to change, we should return to our daily life a bit more refreshed, intrigued, and, maybe on occasion, even a little more excited about new, unforeseen possibilities that have or will come to the fore.

For this to happen, we must learn to be clearer with ourselves, not solely attached to one focus in life. We must use panoramic psychological lenses if a healthy perspective is to grow and deepen in our lives and those we stand alongside. With such an attitude, we will recognize that feeling intolerant of others and their views has no place. But more than that, we will realize that harsh judgment and intolerance of our own actions and feelings have no place either, for they lead only to a darkness (denial, avoidance, cognitive distortion) that will limit our vision... *and our lives.*

A healthy perspective is worth all the effort. It is both the psychological pearl of great price and the calm in the storm. And so, it is worth continued study and commitment. And if this seems too hard or impractical, let us recall from the introduction the mentor's question previously posed, "How much effort does it take to open up your eyes to see?" In addition, as psychologist and spiritual guide Henri Nouwen noted in his most academic work, *Reaching Out,*

> When we think back to the places where we felt most at home, we quickly see that it was where our hosts gave us the precious freedom to come and go on our own terms and did not claim us for their own needs. Only in a free space can re-creation take place and new life be found. The real host is one who offers that space where we do not have to be afraid and where we can listen to our own inner voices and find our own personal way of being human. But to be such a host we have to first of all be at home in our own house.

This book has been about being more "at home" with ourselves through seeking, gaining, and regaining a healthier perspective. As we do this, we begin more and more to recognize what a gift life is and what a wonderful gift it is to share. And it doesn't get any better than that.

APPENDIX

Once Through the Portals: Daily Reflections on Reinforcing a Healthy Perspective

In her edited work *Paris Was Ours*, journalist and critic Penelope Rowlands joins thirty-one other writers to reminisce about their time in France as expatriates. One of the points she—and others—put forth was the impact that being in Paris had on them in both obvious and lasting ways. She writes,

> Just as Indians under British colonial rule entered a new social category after studying in the British Isles—becoming categorized ever afterward as "England-returned"…the rest of us who have spent time in Paris, succeeding there in spite of cultural differences we'd hardly known existed before, were deeply, permanently changed by the experience. We, the Paris-returned, *are* different, in ways large and small. We may

have—mercifully!—stopped talking about foulards at some point, but we still knotted our scarves differently in the end. (And that's just the part of us that you can see....)

Similarly, the search for a healthy perspective, and experiences encountered when we have it, can impact us in ways both obvious and subtle, *forever.*

With a healthy perspective, life can be filled with promise and mystery: promise because it broadens our mental horizon and mystery because it awakens new intuitive wisdom through a true sense of openness. With this in mind, this book has been designed to explore new experiences in the search for a healthier perspective, including the following:

- Appreciating that having a healthy perspective is truly the pearl of great price because it produces greater inner space to truly and fully enjoy what is already in our lives and to welcome what enters each day. It is also the calm within the storm because with a healthy perspective, faithfulness and presence to others becomes more possible since we are not doing it primarily to be successful, have others follow our suggestions or out of duty or guilt.
- Respecting and honoring silence, solitude, and alonetime not simply as means of renewal—although that they are as well—but also as "places" for self-discovery and self-compassion.
- Expanding our sense of self through an appreciation of some of the key principles of positive psychology and cognitive behavioral, schema, and narrative therapies.

- Exploring gratefulness and happiness from new vantage points so more can be extracted from our brief lives.
- Fathoming the new findings on posttraumatic growth so that after experiencing a significant loss, stress, or trauma, we will greet and embrace these opportunities in the best way possible to become deeper, more compassionate people.
- Understanding a myriad of ways to overcome resistance to openness and change so a healthier perspective, way of living, and sharing ourselves becomes more possible.
- Permeating our lives with a sense of *intrigue* (rather than being simply judgmental) about the way we view ourselves and life.
- Shifting from a focus on the external to a nonpunitive or nonjudgmental embrace of our own role. In this way, we can tap into our inner power to color our lives in new ways such as through a more mindful, sensory experience of all that is in front of us; experience new autonomy; develop a broader array of problem-solving skills; cease our avoidance of growth and change because we fear the pain that might be involved; appreciate the existential need for new meaning making; and have greater faith in our own wisdom.

When these goals are put in place, the very act of being involved in the process of seeking a healthier perspective allows us to return to each new day a bit more refreshed and a little more intrigued. Knowing that the wisdom within us is yet to be explored is like being in the deep water just off a barrier reef with no end in sight for what we shall encounter. To help accomplish this, by way of closing this brief book, the following reflections are offered to take into each upcoming day as callings to a new way of seeing...and living. How we use them, of course, is up to us.

A suggestion I would offer is to read one in the morning, see what instantly seems striking, and then place that reaction as a nest in your day—one that can be returned to in a quiet moment between calls, on the way to getting a cup of coffee, or during the drive to and from work.

In one of Billy Collins's poems ("Introduction to Poetry" in his collection *Sailing Alone Around the Room*), he reflects on how new students of poetry seek to interpret the poems put before them. He suggests holding them up to the light, like a slide, or lightly encountering them in different ways. Yet, he feels like new students begin beating the poem with a hose to find out what it really might mean. I laughed as I read the poem about both his invitation to enjoy and explore poetry and the unproductive way many seek to find its core. I think my laughter was all the richer because I have done just that in the past.

The same can be said about "reflections"; gentleness belongs alongside the desire for clarity and personal relevance. So, in moving to this final section of the book, above all, I do wish for a gentle spirit in exploring them.

I believe everyone has had to confront hard times. Trauma, loss, defeat, and suffering have found all of us—sometimes at possibly very vulnerable times. From these dark periods, some of us rise out of the ashes more sensitive to the pure gift of life and become more compassionate toward the plight of others. Such an occurrence doesn't just happen, of course. Such an attitude toward life and the needs of others is borne out of attention to what is important and true, and requires a commitment to act on such learning. Is it any wonder, then, that the classic wisdom literature and current psychological findings all point to the noble results of such a process? It is certainly one worth reinforcing through daily reflection, and I offer the following prompts to forming a healthier perspective as a way of beginning a personal dialogue on the types of themes discussed in this book.

REFLECTIONS ON PERSPECTIVE

Traversing the transitions in our lives is just as important as the actual entry into those new developmental phases we will remain in for a period of time. Since this is so, we must face our places of movement and mystery with a sense of gentleness and a recognition that confusion is part of the process of life, so we must resist seeking quick answers to profound questions that come with changes in life. In the words of naturalist Peter Matthiessen in his book *Nine-Headed Dragon River,* "It is difficult to adjust because I do not know who is adjusting: I am no longer that old person and not yet the new." That is the state of things that must be honored as we begin to appreciate and seek to gain a healthier perspective. Rushing the transition will not produce the insight any more quickly. In fact, the opposite might take place, and the old axiom "The faster I go, the behinder I get" might apply to us. Pacing and patience, though not necessarily honored today, are part of the marathon of life. Confusion, rather than being bad, may be one of the early signs that we are now more awake to the transition that has just begun for us.

When we make space for alonetime we are able to sit with many questions that call us to wake up. Included in them certainly is the question "What remains *unlived* and *unclaimed* in my life?"

Having a healthy perspective often isn't so much about grasping something new as it is being willing and able to let go of something familiar. Once the space is there, then what is fresh will find us.

At the very least, in being more mindful in life, we will find many things we have long enjoyed to be more flavorful. That's what paying attention to what is in front of us provides. (Try it with something small, like your morning coffee or shower.)

When we are acting with a healthy perspective, our compassionate efforts—and our expectations of their results—change radically. We don't have expectations of success or of people trusting us. Instead, we simply seek to be faithful friends who seek to communicate to others our trust in them to make their own decisions for themselves.

In reaching out to others under great stress, we remember to take alonetime so their issues don't contaminate our spirit and so that we, in turn, don't contaminate others with a sense of despair, helplessness, and futility.

When we feel impatient, this is a good signal to us to lean back and reflect on how our own drivenness has crept into the process. We can refresh and reignite our spirit, since it is probably overdue anyway.

When we outgrow the rules of our parents or people in our community, it doesn't necessarily mean we dislike them. It may just mean that our perspective is different now, and maybe it should be. Perhaps it has grown, which is good.

Self-awareness is an ongoing, dynamic undertaking that requires daily attention. When we have a regular process of reflection and mindfulness in place, we can become more attuned to the rhythm of our personality and have our "psychological fingers" on the pulse of where we are emotionally with respect to an issue, person, challenge, or the general thrust of our life's trajectory. To accomplish this, we must take time out to become aware of the ebb and flow of our reactions to note the sometimes subtle inconsistencies between our affect (experiences of sadness, depression, happiness, confusion), our cognitions (ways of thinking, perceiving, and understanding), and our actions. This can provide us with a link to some of the motivations and mental agendas that may presently lie just beyond our awareness and be stymieing our desire for a healthier perspective.

Rather than seeking to avoid difficulties, we can use them as a way to both learn and understand ourselves more deeply.

Challenges are teachers when we don't deny, avoid, or defend against them.

Working on an aspect of ourselves that doesn't seem to permanently change is still a good undertaking because of what, at the very least, it can instill in us: *humility*.

We should learn to laugh at ourselves more readily; it will melt any pretense or pomposity that interferes with reflecting about unpleasant events and foolish things we may have done. It can also help us relax and learn more, rather than involving us in games of self-defense or projection that cut off or distort the helpful conversations we can and should have with ourselves.

When feeling very invested or intense about something, we can recognize this as a red flag, reminding us to ask what gains or fears may also be prompting our attachment to our views or opinions on the issue at hand.

Selfishness, fear, and ignorance may seem to come as friends to protect us, but they are really guards preventing us from going through the portals of new self-knowledge and wisdom in the ongoing search for a healthier perspective.

Letting go is difficult because people think they may lose something. (Poet Donald Hall used to tease that instead of "Live Free or Die," New Hampshire license plates should read "It might come in handy.") Letting go, though, is not about losing something but about being open to receiving what is fresh, new, and more relevant to us in the present situation.

Reflections at the end of the day to decompress provide a chance to empty ourselves of our emotions; allow us to look at our ways of thinking, perceiving, and understanding a situation as a way of uncovering and addressing any dysfunctional/negative cognitions/beliefs; and to enable us to integrate new learning into our personal life.

Rather than throw away personal faults, we can uncover the gifts to which they are attached. Swiss psychiatrist Carl Jung used to remind people that the greater the light, the deeper the darkness. If we are talented in certain ways, then certainly the defensive (exaggerated) side of those talents will show themselves at times as well. An important step to take is not to try to get rid of faults—after all, where will they be disposed of since they are an intermittent part of us? Instead, it is essential to uncover those situations in which our very talents become faults and cause unnecessary pain. For example, when we feel insecure instead of being excited about the gifts we have to enjoy and share, we may have a tendency in the moment to become exhibitionistic.

Normal sadness can teach us when it rises to the surface. Although much has been written on psychological depression, until recently, little has been presented on "normal sadness." Yet, it is a periodic phenomenon everyone faces, and if it is handled adeptly rather than simply draining our energy, it can also help us to appreciate the promise of what new clarity and knowledge can emerge from facing it in the most helpful way. For instance, we may feel the glimmer of sadness during silent periods. The goal in such cases is not to shunt these feelings aside but to greet them like gates gently opening to provide new awareness.

Signs that we are resisting help from mentors, coaches, and informal guides include failing to pay attention to what wise people are trying to tell us, refusing to admit a need for any assistance, needlessly arguing, and not bringing up the very issues that remain the thorniest.

Times when we are most open represent ideal opportunities for growth, change, and broadening our perspective by recognizing that

- our suffering is helping us change the balance of power from staying the same to moving away from the status quo to some new psychological place;
- becoming in tune with the excitement of where new openness and a healthier perspective will lead us is an encouraging experience worth embracing;
- feeling new courage and stamina allows us to face directly self-defeating behavior and the thoughts that underlie it; and
- being truly intrigued about what "secondary gain" (what reinforcement or "advantages") we receive from staying the same is a major step to letting go and moving in new directions.

It is important to have the right circle of friends to challenge, support, tease, and inspire us since the process of overcoming resistances to gaining a healthier perspective can be sabotaged or significantly aided by people in our environment.

In undertaking a personal self-debriefing, we can learn from an emotionally charged event by using a simple rational emotive therapy (RET) approach: (1) choose an occurrence that seemed to stand out for negative or positive reasons; (2) distinguish between what rational and irrational beliefs we might have about it; (3) look at the consequence of thinking/labeling it as we have; (4) dispute our irrational thoughts; and (5) be open to developing a new perspective on it.

We can reinforce new, healthier perspectives in the following ways:

- Being fascinated with the process of finding new ways of viewing our life
- Recognizing that even if we initially fail, participating in activities that increase a healthier perspective are more life-giving and pleasurable than remaining stagnant
- Staying open to new ideas, possibilities, and experiences as part of the movement toward gaining, regaining, or maintaining a healthier perspective can result in surprises, an ability to delay gratification, and helping us deal with frustration—even if the dramatic new insights that are hoped for don't materialize
- Appreciating that our own irrational beliefs are hypotheses, not facts, and can therefore can be examined, disputed, and released
- Being very stubborn about our own refusal to make ourselves miserable about things we can't control now
- Remembering that when opening ourselves to new perspectives, we need to catch ourselves when we feel intimidated

by what *most* people are doing or authorities are saying is the only way to do something/see a situation

---

We need to examine emotions as an archeologist would carefully examine bones during a "dig" because when partially hidden (suppressed/avoided/denied) feelings are brought to the surface, they provide wonderful clues as to where the emotional center of gravity—around which a great deal of our conscious and unconscious attention and energy are orbiting—actually is.

A healthy perspective allows us to increase our awareness of *all* of our agendas and motives. Thinking that we do things for only one reason is naïve. In most cases, there are a number of reasons we do things—some immature, others mature. When we have a more complete awareness of our motives, chances are that the defensive motivations will atrophy while the healthy outlook will be afforded the "psychological space" to grow and deepen. But to accomplish this goal, we must first simultaneously accept that we have very positive objectives in the sharing of our talents and we also, at times, are defensive or egocentric in some unique way.

One of the givens for those people with a healthy perspective is the recognition of the power that cognitions have: they can make a hell of heaven or a heaven of hell. For them, and for us if we wish, negative or disruptive emotions are wonderful red flags that remind us to look at how we are thinking, perceiving, and understanding something rather than readily accepting the impression that we know why we are feeling a particular way.

Simplicity helps us see when our ego is drawing us into dysfunctional thinking and an unhealthy perspective on life. As Ricard notes in his book *Happiness,* "Simplifying one's life to extract its quintessence is the most rewarding... of pursuits. It doesn't mean giving up what is truly beneficial, but finding out what really matters and what brings lasting fulfillment, joy, serenity, and, above all, the irreplaceable boon of altruistic love. It means transforming oneself to better transform the world."

A healthy perspective is not a technique—it is an *attitude* that we give birth to each day when we do the following: take a little alonetime to center and reflect; appreciate that happiness doesn't come from the outside; remind ourselves that gratitude is an approach to life that draws from it so much that exists but is often missed; encourage a willingness to own, rejoice in, and share our signature strengths; and reinforce a desire to reflect, not as a way to be preoccupied with ourselves but to ensure the narrative we have about ourselves is as robust as it can be.

Suffering is often associated with outside events or things that happen to us. Persons who have a healthy perspective on life are convinced otherwise. They see suffering as being a range that can be minimized by looking with a sense of intrigue (rather than self-condemnation) at our egoism, ignorance, attachments, selfishness, and denial that everything changes over time.

When we view compassion correctly, we

- don't worry about success that we can't produce in other people's lives;

- value faithfulness, rather than a need to succeed even in good ways, as the most important aspect of reaching out to others (the archer who thinks of the prize runs a greater chance of missing the target); and
- appreciate that "getting out of ourselves" is very beneficial to having a healthy perspective rather than having some things/events/relationships hurt or destroyed by unhelpful over-self-involvement.

Seeking a healthy perspective each day involves having fun in examining our opinions and views. In doing this, we appreciate that there are many accurate ways something can be viewed. Once again, Matthieu Ricard beautifully points this out when he shared the following Buddhist canonical verse in his book *Happiness*:

> For the lover, a beautiful woman is an object of desire.
> For the hermit, a distraction.
> For the wolf, a good meal.

A continual process of enhancing a healthy perspective can be an exciting, ongoing pilgrimage to find greater direction, meaning, and peace in life. As soon as we feel we have arrived, forgetting that the journey never ends, we cease having a healthy attitude. There is no retirement from this inspirational, and sometimes challenging, journey toward gaining a healthy perspective.

When we take a few moments at the end of the workday—in our office, on the walk to the car, on the drive home, or in our own kitchen—to get in touch with our emotions and respond to our cognitions, we can empty out, learn and renew, as well as lessen the chances that we will be contaminated by our reactions to the day's events. We will also be in a better position to decrease the chances we will contaminate with negativity those we encounter when we return home.

A "tyranny of hope" occurs when we have goals for others that are impossible/impractical for them to reach given their personal and other resources. We need to have *low expectations and high hopes.* This allows us to face people with kindness and clarity, gives them space to move with life as they will, and enables us to avoid feeling negative if they don't respond as we might like them to.

Many problems can be helped to heal through *gratitude.*

The causes of many problems usually involve, to some degree, *ingratitude.*

Nostalgia for the past and the desire for something in the future are not ideal bedfellows for mindfulness or a healthy perspective. Yet, society seems to invest a great deal in getting us to expend energy (and money) to psychologically hopscotch between these two emotional refugees—when, in reality, they only "protect" us from experiencing life in front of us to the fullest. Strange.

A healthy perspective allows us to have enough inner safety to move from avoidance and denial to the point where we can entertain, then resign ourselves to, and eventually accept everything we experience. In this way, we can learn lessons that help us to fathom all there is to experience, enjoy, and share in the brief time we are alive.

When we find that things don't turn out as we would like, Jack Kornfield, in his book *A Path with Heart,* suggests we seek a healthier perspective by asking ourselves simple questions such as these:

How have I treated this difficulty so far?
How have I suffered by my own response and reaction to it?
What does this problem ask me to let go of?
What suffering is unavoidable, is my measure to accept?
What great lessons might it be able to teach me?
What is gold, the value, hidden in this situation?

How do we know we are "getting it" and have a healthy perspective? When we open one "psychological hand," we still see our old habits, growing edges, limits, and defense. When we open the other, we see freedom to really live our lives less hampered by the past and a culture that is stingy with joy, while offering to sell us an inner peace it can't deliver, at a cost that is too high. Maybe seeing what is in both hands *simultaneously* is part of gaining a healthy perspective.

People will often say, I like this or do not like this. But with a healthy perspective, while people will still of course have preferences, their question instead will be, What can I find and be taught in this experience whether I initially like it or not?

Openness is an essential part of catching ourselves when we are playing defensive games. In Clark Strand's *The Wooden Bowl,* he relates the following story to make his point: "A certain yoga teacher once told me that the perfectly enlightened mind was one in which all the knots and kinks and coils had come undone. 'How do you do that?' I asked her. I expected her to explain some sort of postural technique. But she only laughed and said, 'Stop tying knots.'"

One of the enemies of a healthy perspective is overconcern about the opinions of others and how they might view us. In his enjoyable, thought-provoking book on the teachings provided by classic spiritual interchanges between a disciple and a master from an array of spiritual traditions (*One Minute Wisdom*), Anthony de Mello offers the following brief story:

> The Master seemed quite impervious to what people thought of him. When the disciples asked how he had attained this stage of inner freedom, he laughed aloud and said, "Till I was twenty I did not care what people thought of me. After twenty I worried endlessly about what my neighbors thought. Then one day after fifty I suddenly saw that they hardly ever thought of me at all!"

A healthy perspective allows us to accept the invitation to act more spontaneously and see things "outside the box." This is so because freedom is one of its fruits. In her book *Contentment*, Gillian Stokes relates the following simple, but moving, story (and suggestion) to illustrate this:

> [A] wonderful unscripted Parisian moment: a suited businessman crossing one of the many squares in Paris encountered

children playing ping-pong on an outdoor table. Irresistibly drawn, he took off his jacket, placed it with his briefcase on a bench, and politely joined the game. He played with spirit for ten minutes or so, then returned to his jacket, his briefcase, and his office. Pure gold.

Allow yourself to flow with the unexpected and increase your chances of discovering contentment. Organize and plan the skeleton of what you intend, then leave room for pleasant surprises; discover what the universe has made available for you.

There are many portals into new learning for us. Once again, as Marcel Proust notes, "The real voyage consists not in seeking new landscapes, but in having new eyes." And so, a healthy perspective is the pearl of great price because while we can't completely change the world into what we would like or think it should be, we can alter the way we view it. And, when this change occurs in us each day, as a natural matter of course in a gentle, faithful way, we will be in a better position to spontaneously open up a space for others, especially when their lives are stormy.

In Alexandra Fuller's memoir *Cocktail Hour under the Tree of Forgetfulness,* she recalls returning to Africa with her family: "And as the ship veered around the tip of Africa, Mum held me up to the earthy, wood-fire-spiced air. A hot African wind blew my black bowl cut into a halo. 'Smell that,' Mum whispered in my ear. 'That's home.'" I feel the same way when I experience—especially during alonetime—a healthier perspective than I have had in the past. For me, that's home.

REFERENCES

Boldt, M. (2004). *Pursuing human strengths: A positive psychology guide.* New York: Worth.

Braza, J. (1997). *Moment by moment.* Tokyo: Tuttle.

Brazier, D. (1995). *Zen therapy.* Hoboken, NJ: John Wiley & Sons.

Buck, T., & Wicks, R. (2012). Modern positive psychology and formation: Unearthing the gifts and graces of the people of God and those called to servant leadership. *Human Development, 33*(3), 3–7.

Buckingham, M., & Clifton, D. (2001). *Now discover your strengths.* New York: Free Press.

Carr, A. (2004). *Positive psychology: The science of happiness and human strengths.* New York: Routledge.

Collins, B. (2002). *Sailing alone around the room.* New York: Random House.

Covey, S. (2004). *The 7 habits of highly successful people.* New York: Free Press.

Crane, G. (2000). *Bones of the master.* New York: Bantam.

Csikszentmihalyi, M. (1990). *Flow.* New York: Harper.

de Mello, A. (1986). *One minute wisdom.* New York: Doubleday.

Diener, E. (2009). Positive psychology: Past, present, and future. In S. J. Lopez & C. R. Snyder (Eds.), *Oxford handbook of positive psychology* (2nd ed., pp. 7–12). New York: Oxford University Press.

Diener, E., & Diener, R. (2009). *Happiness.* New York: John Wiley & Sons.

Dillard, A. (1989). *The writing life.* New York: Harper & Row.

du Boulay, S. (1998). *Beyond the darkness.* New York: Doubleday.

Emerson, R. W. (1965). *The selected writings of Ralph Waldo Emerson.* London: Penguin Books.

Emmons, R. (2007). *Thanks!* Boston: Houghton-Mifflin.

Evans, H. (2009). *Paper chase.* New York: Little-Brown.

Frankl, V. (1984). *Man's search for meaning.* New York: Washington Square Press.

Fredrickson, B. (1998). "What good are positive emotions?" *Review of General Psychology, 2,* 300–319.

Fredrickson, B. (2009). *Positivity.* New York: Three Rivers Press.

Frey, D., & Schmook, R. (1995). Ideemanagement. Strategien zur optimierung und aktivierung des betrieblichen vorschlagswesen. In *Personalfuhrung, 28*(2), S. 116–125.

Fuller, A. (2011). *Cocktail hour under the tree of forgetfulness.* New York: Penguin.

Fulton, P. (2005). Mindfulness as clinical training. In C. Germer, R. Siegel, & P. Fulton (Eds.), *Mindfulness and psychotherapy* (pp. 55–72). New York: Guilford Press.

Germer, C. (2009). *The mindful path to self-compassion.* New York: Guilford Press.

Germer, C., Siegel, R., & Fulton, P. (Eds.). (2005). *Mindfulness and psychotherapy.* New York: Guilford Press.

Hanh, Thich Nhat. (1989, November/December). Seeding the

unconscious: New views on Buddhism and psychotherapy. *Common Boundary, 7*(6), 14–21.

Hauser, R. (2000). The minister and personal prayer. In R. Wicks (Ed.), *Handbook of spirituality for ministers, Vol. 2* (pp. 375–395). Mahwah, NJ: Paulist Press.

Hemingway, E. (2009). *A moveable feast.* New York: Simon & Schuster.

Hodges, T., & Clifton, D. (2004). Strengths-based development in practice. In P. Linely & S. Josephs (Eds.), *Positive psychology in practice* (pp. 256–268). Hoboken, NJ: John Wiley & Sons.

hooks, b. (2000). *All about love.* New York: Morrow.

Housden, R. (2001). *Ten poems to save your life.* New York: Harmony.

Iyer, P. (2008). *The open road: The global journey of the fourteenth Dalai Lama.* New York: Knopf.

Kierkegaard, S. (1987). *Either/or.* Princeton, NJ: Princeton University Press.

Kornfield, J. (1993). *A path with heart.* New York: Bantam.

Kornfield, J. (2000). *After the ecstasy, the laundry.* New York: Bantam.

Krishnamurti, J. (1963). *Life ahead: On learning and search for meaning.* Novato, CA: New World Library.

Lawrence, D. H. 2003. *The Cambridge edition of the works of D. H. Lawrence.* Cambridge: Cambridge University Press.

Madigan, S. (2011). *Narrative therapy.* Washington, DC: American Psychological Association.

Maitland, S. (2008). *A book of silence.* Berkeley, CA: Counterpoint.

Matthiessen, P. (1986). *Nine-headed dragon river.* Boston: Shambala.

May, G. (2005). *The dark night of the soul: A psychiatrist explores the connection between darkness and spiritual growth.* San Francisco: HarperOne.

McLain, P. (2012). *The Paris wife.* New York: Ballantine.

Merton, T. (1988). *A vow of conversation.* New York: Farrar, Straus and Giroux.

Merton, T. Quoted in Mott, M. (1984). *The seven mountains of Thomas Merton*. Boston: Houghton-Mifflin.

Mott, M. (1984). *The seven mountains of Thomas Merton*. Boston: Houghton-Mifflin.

Neimeyer, R. A. (2000). Narrative disruptions in the construction of the self. In R. A. Neimeyer & J. D. Raskin (Eds.), *Constructions of disorder: Meaning-making frameworks for psychotherapy* (pp. 207–242). Washington, DC: American Psychological Association.

Neimeyer, R. A. (Ed.). (2001). *Meaning reconstruction and the experience of loss*. Washington, DC: American Psychological Association.

Norris, K. (1993). *Dakota: A spiritual geography*. New York: Riverhead.

Nouwen, H. (1975). *The Genesee diary*. New York: Doubleday.

Nouwen, H. (1975). *Reaching out*. New York: Doubleday.

Nouwen, H. (1981). *The way of the heart*. New York: Seabury/Harper.

Offer, A. (2007). *The challenge of affluence*. New York: Oxford University Press.

Palmer, P. (2000). *Let your life speak*. San Francisco: Jossey-Bass.

Park, C. (2004). The notion of growth following stressful life experiences: Problems and prospects. *Psychological Inquiry, 15*, 69–76.

Park, C. (2005). Religion as a meaning-making framework in coping with life stress. *Journal of Social Issues, 61*, 707–729.

Park, C. (2005). Religion and meaning. In R. Paloutzain & C. Parks (Eds.), *Handbook of psychology and religion* (pp. 295–313). New York: Guilford Press.

Park, C. (2008). Testing the meaning-making model of coping with loss. *Journal of Social and Clinical Psychology, 27*, 970–994.

Penny, L. (2011). *A trick of the light*. New York: Minotaur Books.

Percy, W. (1998). *The moviegoer*. New York: Vintage.

Peterson, C. (2006). *A primer on positive psychology*. New York: Oxford University Press.

Peterson, C., & Seligman, M. (2004). *Character strengths and virtues classification system.* New York: Oxford University Press.

Prather, H. (1998). In D. Salwak. *The wonders of solitude.* New York: New World Library.

Prochnik, G. (2010). *In pursuit of silence: Listening for meaning in a world of noise.* New York: Doubleday.

Proust, M. (1987). *La prisonniere.* Paris: Gaillimard.

Ricard, M. (2003). *Happiness: A guide to developing life's most important skill.* New York: Little, Brown.

Rilke, R. (1954/2004). *Letters to a young poet.* New York: W. W. Norton.

Ritter, C. (1954/2010). *A woman in the polar night.* Fairbanks: University of Alaska Press.

Rowlands, P. (Ed.). (2011). *Paris was ours.* Chapel Hill, NC: Algonquin Press.

Ryff, C. (1989). Happiness is everything, or is it? Explorations on the meaning of psychological well-being. *Journal of Personality and Social Psychology, 57,* 1069–1081.

Seligman, M. (2002). *Authentic happiness: Using positive psychology to realize your potential for lasting fulfillment.* New York: Free Press.

Steindl-Rast, D. (1984). *Gratefulness, the heart of prayer: An approach to life in fullness.* Mahwah, NJ: Paulist Press.

Stevenson, R. (2009). *An apology for idlers.* London: Penguin Books.

Stokes, G. (2002). *Contentment: Wisdom from around the world.* Philadelphia, PA: Red Wheel.

Storr, E. (1988). *Solitude.* New York: Bantam.

Strand, C. (1988). *The wooden bowl.* New York: Hyperion.

Thoreau, H. (1854/1955). *Walden pond; or, life in the woods.* New York: Dover.

White, M., & Epston, D. (1990). *Narrative means to therapeutic ends.* New York: Norton.

Wicks, R. (2000). (Ed.). *Handbook of spirituality for ministers, Vol. 2.* Mahwah, NJ: Paulist Press.

Wicks, R. (2010). *Bounce: Living the resilient life.* New York: Oxford University Press.

Wicks, R. (2010). *Simple changes.* Notre Dame, IN: Sorin Books.

Wicks, R. (2011). *Streams of contentment.* Notre Dame, IN: Sorin Books.

Wicks, R. (2012). *The inner life of the counselor.* Hoboken, NJ: John Wiley & Sons.

Wicks, R., & Buck, T. (2011). Reframing for change: The use of cognitive behavioral therapy and positive psychology in pastoral ministry and formation. *Human Development, 32*(3), 8–14.

Yalom, I. (1980). *Existential psychotherapy.* New York: Basic Books.

Yen, S. (2008). *Footprints in the snow.* New York: Bantam.

READING A BIT FURTHER

Some of the topics touched on in this book may have struck you as particularly relevant. Following are some suggested readings for each chapter. They, in turn, will lead you even further though both contents and their sources/bibliographies.

Chapter 1: Mindfulness

Practically any book on mindfulness will offer you the basics on the overall approach to be in the now with attentiveness and openness. Among the ones I have found the most useful are Braza, *Moment by Moment*; Germer, *The Mindful Path to Self-Compassion*; Gunaratana, *Mindfulness in Plain English*; Hahn, *The Miracle of Mindfulness*; Kabat-Zinn, *Wherever You Go, There You Are*; Kornfield, *A Path with Heart*; Langer, *Mindfulness*; Strand, *The*

Wooden Bowl; and Suzuki, *Zen Mind, Beginner's Mind.* I have a section on mindfulness in my own book *Bounce: Living the Resilient Life,* that may also be of interest.

Chapter 2: Positive Psychology and Narrative Therapy

With respect to positive psychology, there are numerous books out on the topic. Of particular interest are Fredrickson, *Positivity*; Csikszentmihalyi, *Flow*; Pearsall, *The Beethoven Factor*; and Peterson, *A Primer on Positive Psychology*. Other books that might be of interest are Frisch, *Quality of Life Therapy*; *Well-Being,* edited by Kahneman, Diener, and Schwarz; and *Flourishing,* edited by Keyes and Haidt.

With respect to narrative therapy, there are a number of books for professionals on the topic, including *Narrative Therapy: The Archaeology of Hope,* edited by Monk, Winslade, Crocket, and Epston; and *Narrative Therapy: The Social Construction of Preferred Realities,* by Jill Freedman and Gene Combs. They are fairly readable, regardless of whether or not you are a clinician. However, probably the best one to start with is *Narrative Therapy,* by Stephen Madigan.

Chapter 3: Happiness and Gratitude

Although the books on positive psychology touch on both gratefulness and happiness, ones dealing with this specific topic which are most helpful include Emmons, *Thanks!*; Stendl-Rast, *Gratefulness*; Haidt, *The Happiness Hypothesis*; Ricard, *Happiness*; and Seligman, *Authentic Happiness.* They cover the range of both psychology and spirituality of gratefulness and happiness.

Chapter 4: Posttraumatic Growth

In this area, the most prominent book for a general readership is Stephen Joseph's *What Doesn't Kill Us: The New Psychology of Posttraumatic Growth*. Of additional interest may be a book I coauthored with young scholar Mary Beth Werdel titled *A Primer on Posttraumatic Growth*. If you wish to read books by those who pioneered the field, look for works by Tedeschi and Calhoun. In the psychological literature, articles on meaning making by Park may also be of interest.

Chapter 5: Overcoming Resistance to Openness and Change

Brooks and Goldstein's book *The Power of Resilience,* Duhigg's *The Power of Habit,* Burns's *Feeling Good,* Seligman's *What You Can Change and What You Can't,* Young and Klosko's *Reinventing Your Life,* and Wachtel's edited classic *Resistance,* as well as my own brief work *Simple Changes,* may be helpful. In addition, Brazier's *Zen Therapy* and books by psychologist Kornfield on Eastern spirituality (*A Path with Heart; After the Ecstasy, the Laundry;* and *The Wise Heart*) all deal with resistance in creative ways, no matter what your religious belief system may be or whether you have one at all.

ACKNOWLEDGMENTS

For permission to adapt relevant material from several of my books, I wish to thank Sorin Books, John Wiley & Sons, Inc., and *Human Development* magazine.

For suggestions, as well as editorial and/or research assistance, I'd like to acknowledge the comments/work of Laura McKenna, Elizabeth Campbell, Mary Beth Werdel, Brendan Geary, Colin Rhoades, Lisa Marie Tucker, and Theresa Wilkins.

A special note of gratitude goes to Joan Bossert of Oxford University Press for her insightful comments and recommendations—she is the editor and publisher most writers wish for but rarely find. I have been very fortunate, and I know it.

I thank Tina Buck for allowing me to adapt material we worked on conjointly for *Human Development* magazine and for her careful editorial support.

For their support of my work on resilience and maintaining a healthy perspective with the following audiences, I wish to thank Christine Candio, Peter Bernard, Bonnie Shelor, and Maureen McGuire (health care); Robert Bruno, Rick Spencer, and Jim Hamel (military); Mary Catherine Bunting, Russ Roide, Billy Davies, Jim Barker, and Joe Luca (ministry); Therese Borchard, Brad Erford, and Joe Ciarrocchi (counseling and psychology); Edith Prendergast, Jan Pedroza, and Ron Valente (education); Dan Boyd and Wayne Fitzpatrick (relief workers and NGOs [nongovernmental officials] in war-torn areas); and Louisa Hollman (general audience). There are many others who know they have also played a significant part in my efforts to encourage mindfulness, self-care, clear thinking, and compassion—especially among those in the healing and helping professions. Although I have not cited you specifically, please know that I am extremely grateful to you as well.

And, as always, I am extremely indebted to the insightful suggestions of my wife, Michaele, on how to best convey the material included in my books. Thank you again…and *always*.

CREDITS

Buck, T., and Wicks, R. (2012). Modern positive psychology and formation: Unearthing the gifts and graces of the people of God and those called to servant leadership, *Human Development, 33*(3). Reprinted with permission from *Human Development* magazine. Subscription information may be obtained at www.humandevelopmentmag.org.

Germer, C. (2009). *The mindful path to self-compassion.* New York: Guilford. Used with permission of Guildford Press.

Werdel, M., and Wicks, R. (2012). *Primer on posttraumatic growth.* New York: Wiley. Reprinted with permission of John Wiley & Sons, Inc.

Wicks R. (2000). *Prayerfulness.* Notre Dame, IN: Sorin Books. Used by permission of Ave Maria Press.

Wicks, R. (2000). *Simple changes.* Notre Dame, IN: Sorin Books. Used by permission of Ave Maria Press.

Wicks R. (2003). *Riding the dragon.* Notre Dame, IN: Sorin Books. Used by permission of Ave Maria Press.

Wicks, R. (2011). *Streams of contentment.* Notre Dame, IN: Sorin Books. Used by permission of Ave Maria Press.

Wicks, R. (2012). *The inner life of the counselor.* New York: Wiley. Reprinted with permission of John Wiley & Sons.

Wicks, R., & Buck, T. (2011). Reframing for change: The use of cognitive behavioral therapy and positive psychology in pastoral ministry and formation. *Human Development, 32*(3). Reprinted with permission from *Human Development* magazine. Subscription information may be obtained at www.humandevelopmentmag.org.

INDEX